FIGHT NIGHT!

THE THINKING FAN'S GUIDE TO MIXED MARTIAL ARTS

by Lito Angeles

PUNISHMENT
CLOTHING
.COM

FIGHT NIGHT!

THE THINKING FAN'S GUIDE TO MIXED MARTIAL ARTS

by Lito Angeles

Edited by Sarah Dzida, Raymond Horwitz,
Jeannine Santiago and Jon Sattler

Graphic Design by John Bodine

Cover Photo by David Schantz

Models: Tony Cortina and Tate Littlepage

© 2009 Black Belt Communications LLC
All Rights Reserved
Printed in Korea
Library of Congress Control Number: 2009922510
ISBN-10: 0-89750-175-6
ISBN-13: 978-0-89750-175-0

First Printing 2009

BLACK BELT BOOKS
A Division of **OHARA** PUBLICATIONS, INC.
World Leader in Martial Arts Publications

ACKNOWLEDGMENTS

Janine, Alyssa, Ryan and Kiana
Thank you for your unconditional love and encouragement in all I do. I dedicate this book to you. Abe, Rosemarie, Digna, Lisa, Joe, Carlito, Gabe and Jackie, thank you for your love and support.

Robert W. Young
Thank you for your friendship and all the opportunities you've given me over the years. You've allowed me to indulge in my passion. I am indebted …

Tony Cortina and Tate Littlepage
Thank you for being my "fall guys."

Sarah Dzida, Raymond Horwitz, Jeannine Santiago and Jon Sattler
Thank you for the incredible editing you did with my book.

John Bodine
Thank you for the awesome design that you created for my book.

Bas Rutten
Thank you for writing the foreword.

Don Walter
Thank you for the assistance you provided me on the history of the mixed martial arts.

FOREWORD

In October 1996, I came to America from Japan to see if my wife and I could build a life here.

During that trip, I taught a seminar for the Los Angeles Police Department's Arrest and Control Unit, and it was there that I first met Lito Angeles, who was one of the unit's master instructors.

Years later, we would meet again when Lito did a three-part interview on me for *Black Belt*. It was at that moment that we connected and I learned more about this interesting individual.

Lito is someone who can do a lot of different things and do them well. He understands the "big 4"—boxing, *muay Thai*, wrestling and Brazilian *jiu-jitsu*, and because he really understands these styles, he's also good at "carrying it over" to people who don't.

There is a huge difference between knowing something and teaching it, and Lito gets that, so besides the fact that he can handle himself in dangerous situations, he also knows how to teach it, and that's a rare quality.

Fight Night! The Thinking Fan's Guide to Mixed Martial Arts is a great book for understanding sport MMA. Lito clearly shows how techniques are effective when used properly. Simply do what he shows you to do, and your sparring partner/opponent will tap!

MMA has come a long way since I started competing in September 1993 in Japan. Finally, we see more fighters who can knock their opponents out or submit them when the opportunity presents itself because they cross-train. These fighters are truly mixed martial artists.

Last words: This is a great book in which you can reference many situations found in MMA, but everybody knows that "practice makes perfect." So find yourself a good training partner and off you go …

One last thing, always make sure you are in shape so that your mind/body connection works flawless.

Be safe and Godspeed.

—Bas Rutten
2009

PREFACE

I first fell in love with the martial arts in 1972 with the Bruce Lee movie *The Chinese Connection* (aka. *Fist of Fury*). A few years later, in 1975, I began training in *shorin-ryu* karate while my father was stationed in Japan. Over the ensuing years, I've studied Western boxing, Western wrestling, *jeet kune do*, *kali*, *escrima*, *boxe Francaise savate*, *pentjak silat*, *muay Thai*, *krav maga*, Brazilian *jiu-jitsu* and the Real Combat System because I've always had an interest in mixing martial arts. I've won competitions in a few of these systems and dabbled in a host of others. In addition, as a police officer, I've also had my fair share of real-world street encounters.

Anyway, from that fateful day in 1972 to the present and foreseeable future, my passion for the martial arts has flourished. I'm an avid researcher, practitioner and instructor as well as a contributing writer for *Black Belt* magazine since 1998. I've used all my knowledge and experiences to bring you the essential elements that define the mixed martial arts. I am proud and honored to have this opportunity to share my love for the sport, and I thank you for reading it.

—Lito Angeles
2009

NSAC

ou

TABLE OF CONTENTS

INTRODUCTION

If you are a fan of mixed martial arts, this book is for you. This primer breaks down the most commonly used MMA techniques, terms and tactics. While not a be-all and end-all encyclopedia detailing every move in MMA, it contains the most popular, well-known ones and will give you a better understanding of the moves you're watching or performing.

While this is not an instructional book, it contains a fairly detailed breakdown of the techniques. And who knows? Maybe it will inspire you to take up mixed martial arts.

I wrote this book because MMA is one of the most exciting sports in the world and I'd like to help spread the "word" to the masses. For pure, unadulterated athleticism and all-out action, mixed martial arts is the most compelling combat sport around. No other sport, combat-oriented or otherwise, matches the purity and totality of mixed-martial arts competition. There are no balls, bats, clubs, pucks, rackets, nets, goals or end zones. In short, there is no external equipment whatsoever aside from gloves for protection and cages and rings to keep the action confined. Instead, mixed martial arts uses the human body's natural weapons with skill and technique for competition.

This is what makes MMA so special. My goal is to make you a bigger fan of MMA and inspire you to become more involved in this awesome combative sport. OK, enough said. Enjoy the book.

WHAT IS MIXED MARTIAL ARTS?

Before delving into the terms, it's appropriate to start things off by defining what mixed martial arts is and isn't.

Despite what many people believe, MMA is not a barbaric blood sport. It is a stringently regulated combat sport that attracts among the highest caliber and all-around well-conditioned athletes in the world. The training regimen of the average professional MMA fighter would thoroughly exhaust most athletes in other sports due in part to its comprehensive nature. Some of you may be thinking, How about the athletes who compete in Olympic decathlons or Ironman triathlons? Well, both of these multi-event sports are very demanding. However, the big difference that separates the two from MMA is that they don't simultaneously apply multilevel skill sets directly against one another to attain victory.

There are three recognized phases of combat in mixed martial arts:

- **Stand-up:** The combatants have space between them and aren't holding each other.

- **Clinch:** The competitors are very close to each other, and their arms and upper bodies are tied up.

- **Ground/grappling:** The fighters are on the mat and their limbs are entangled.

In their never-ending quest to evolve and improve, modern mixed martial artists are well-rounded and well-versed in all phases of combat. It's pretty much a prerequisite these days to be proficient in all phases. With that said, there are still two general categories of MMA fighters: strikers and grapplers. The strikers are fighters who prefer to keep their distance from their opponents so they can dominate fights through punches, kicks, knees and elbow strikes. Their main goal is to knock out their opponents. Conversely, grapplers prefer to close the distance and take their opponents to the ground, where they can either pound their opponents until the referee stops the fight or apply a submission hold.

MMA is an eclectic combination of various martial arts, most notably the big four: Western boxing, *muay Thai*, Western wrestling (such as Greco-Roman, freestyle, folkstyle and catch-as-catch-can) and Brazilian *jiu-jitsu*. Other systems that shape MMA include *sambo*, judo, *sanshou* and, to a lesser extent, various styles of Japanese-based karate. The following list elaborates each style a little more:

- **Western boxing** is a striking art that only uses punches, which are generally divided into jabs, crosses, hooks and uppercuts.

- **Muay Thai** is a Thai-based martial art referred to as "the art of eight limbs." It is a fighting system that uses the fists, elbows, shins, feet and knees to strike an opponent. Combined with Greco-Roman wrestling, muay Thai is also considered the essential clinching art of MMA.

- **Greco-Roman wrestling** is one of the major styles of Western wrestling. It focuses on upper-body attacks and forbids any attack below the waist, even leg takedowns. As a result, clinch work, head locks, bear hugs and throws are prominent aspects of this style.

- **Freestyle wrestling** is one of the major styles of amateur Western wrestling. It allows both upper- and lower-body attacks, which means that leg takedowns and defenses are prominent parts of this style.

- **Folkstyle wrestling** is an indigenous style to the United States. It is basically a hybrid of freestyle wrestling practiced mainly in high schools and colleges.

- **Catch wrestling**, also known as catch-as-catch-can wrestling, is an "old school" submission style of wrestling best known for its brutal submission holds, including leg locks, neck locks, arm locks, shoulder locks and chokeholds.

- **Brazilian jiu-jitsu** focuses on grappling, especially ground fighting. A BJJ competitor's goal is to obtain and maintain a dominant position in order to use a submission hold, like a joint lock or choke, that will force his opponent to submit.

- **Sambo**, also called *sombo*, is a Russian martial art that emphasizes jacketed wrestling and grappling skills in its sport variation. It is widely known for its leg locks.

- **Judo** is a classical Japanese grappling art that primarily emphasizes throws—shoulder throws, hip throws, sweeps, etc.

- **Sanshou** is a full-contact Chinese sport that consists of kickboxing techniques, takedowns and throws.

- **Karate** is a Japanese martial art with numerous styles. It is primarily a punching and kicking system that incorporates, to a lesser degree, many of the other natural weapons of the body for attack and defense.

- *Taekwondo* is a Korean variation of karate that strongly emphasizes kicking.

- **Submission grappling**, also known as submission fighting or submission wrestling, is a martial sport that combines tactics and techniques from Brazilian jiu-jitsu, Western wrestling (all forms), sambo, judo and *luta livre,* (Brazilian freestyle fighting).

Ancient MMA History

The roots of mixed martial arts can be traced back to the Greeks, who introduced the sport of *pankration* into the Olympic Games back in 648 BCE. The name pankration is a derivative of two Greek words: *"pan,"* meaning "all" and *"kratos,"* meaning "powers." The sport was aptly named because it reflected a potent mix of skills from Hellenic boxing and wrestling. Competitors would win by either knocking out or submitting their opponent. Aside from the Spartans, who allowed anything-goes hand-to-hand combat, there were basically two rules that governed the bouts: 1. no biting and 2. no eye gouging.

The techniques utilized by ancient *pankratists* were similar to what is being used today in MMA. The stand-up and clinch phases of combat included punches, kicks, elbow strikes and knee strikes to all parts of the body. In the grappling phase, a wide variety of takedowns, chokes, strangleholds and joint locks were employed. While matches encompassed all phases of unarmed combat, the majority of pankration competitions were finished on the ground. When death resulted, it was more often than not the result of a stranglehold.

Pankration matches took place in a compact square-shaped ring usually 12 to 14 feet across. The ring was purposely kept this small to encourage constant action. In addition, the matches had no time limits, so bouts could last for hours. This brutal test of skills and will made it the most popular Olympic event of its era. Pankration flourished in Greece for centuries, but the rise of the Roman Empire brought about its decline. This in essence brought about the demise of MMA's first incarnation.

Numerous mixed-style matches took place in the late 1800s and early 1900s throughout America, Europe, Japan and the Pacific Rim. Authentic wrestlers representing the catch-as-catch-can and Greco-Roman wrestling styles participated in challenge matches against professional boxers and high-ranking *jujutsu*/judo practitioners. However, the revival of what is now known as mixed martial arts didn't occur until 1925 when the charismatic Gracie family established their *vale tudo* (anything-goes) fighting style in Brazil.

Gracie MMA History

In 1801, George Gracie immigrated to Brazil from Scotland, settling in the Para province on the northeastern side of the country. As the years passed, George flourished in his newly adopted homeland and expanded his family. In the early 1900s, George's grandson Gastão Gracie made a name for himself in politics. Around that time, Mitsuyo Maeda (known as Count Koma in his native country) immigrated to the Para province to establish a Japanese colony for his government. As such, Maeda and Gastão crossed paths and eventually became close friends. Gastão used his influence to help Maeda establish this proposed colony.

To repay Gastão, Maeda offered to teach Gastão's son Carlos the Japanese art of judo.

Besides his political prowess, Maeda was also a renowned judo champion. Gastão accepted, and Maeda taught the 15-year-old Carlos for six years. When Maeda left Brazil to return to his homeland, Carlos began teaching his younger brothers—Jorge, Osvaldo, Gastão Jr. and Helio—the same form of judo that Maeda had shown him. Carlos and Helio eventually began to adapt the art, focusing more on the ground game. In 1925, Carlos and Helio moved to Rio de Janeiro, where they opened up their first jiu-jitsu academy.

In order to generate publicity for their new school, Carlos issued what would become known as the "Gracie Challenge" by placing advertisements in several Rio de Janiero newspapers. The ads contained a picture of the delicate Carlos along with the infamous statement, "If you want a broken arm or rib, contact Carlos Gracie at this number."

This boast triggered a mixed-martial arts renaissance in the Western world. Carlos and Helio took on all challengers in vale tudo matches, which closely resembled ancient pankration competitions. Brazilian martial artists representing many styles took up the challenge, but they were resoundingly defeated by the superior Gracie system.

As their reputation grew, the Gracie Challenge matches transitioned to Brazil's largest soccer stadiums, attracting record crowds. Helio—followed in later years by sons, nephews and relatives like Rickson, Rolls and Carlson—continued defeating all challengers, including professional boxers, wrestlers, *karateka*, *capoeira* stylists and world-renowned Japanese *judoka*.

Helio lost two matches out of the 1,000 he fought between 1935 and 1951. His first defeat was to Masahiko Kimura, arguably the greatest Japanese judoka of all time. Kimura graciously described Helio as the true victor because the match lasted far longer than the judoka had expected. The other loss came from one of his own students, Carlos Santana, in an epic three-hour and 45-minute match, which is still considered to be the longest MMA fight ever.

Through Gracie family efforts, the revived sport of mixed martial arts became immensely popular in Brazil, only surpassed by the country's most popular sport, soccer. When the Gracies realized that their style could make an indelible mark on the martial arts world, Rorion Gracie (Helio's oldest son) made the move to the United States to spread his family's art of Brazilian jiu-jitsu.

In the early 1980s, Rorion settled in Torrance, California, and began teaching Brazilian jiu-jitsu (or as he preferred to call it, "Gracie jiu-jitsu") in the garage of his home. In order to generate widespread publicity for his family's system, he followed in his uncle and father's footsteps and issued the infamous "Gracie Challenge" with a new twist. He offered $100,000 to anyone who could defeat him or one of his brothers in a vale tudo match. Like in the past, a variety of martial artists accepted the challenge and were all defeated. Once again, these matches brought the Gracie family and their brand of jujutsu much notoriety, which they wanted. From these matches, Rorion came up with an idea that would revolutionize both sports and martial arts.

Rorion befriended Art Davie, who had connections in the TV industry. Through these connections, Davie set up a meeting with Bob Meyrowitz and Campbell McLaren, the president and programming director of Semaphore Entertainment Group, a corporation that specialized in broadcasting live pay-per-view sporting events. Rorion and Davie pitched their idea of a vale tudo martial arts tournament, in which experts from various disciplines faced off to determine which martial art was the best. Meyrowitz loved the idea, and the three men established the Ultimate Fighting Championship.

On November 12, 1993, SEG debuted the first UFC. It was supposed to be a one-time event, but the inaugural show generated a surprising 86,000 pay-per-view buys. In the end, the first UFC ushered in the Western-world rebirth of mixed martial arts through its direct connection with the Gracie family.

Modern MMA History

Like the pankratists, early UFC events were advertised as "no-holds-barred" tournaments. This moniker did apply to the first six UFCs, which had very few rules. The only rules in the first six events were no eye gouging, no biting and no fish-hooking, meaning you couldn't hook a finger into an opponent's mouth to manipulate his head. The bouts were fought inside the "octagon," an eight-sided chain-linked cage created by renowned filmmaker Milos Forman. There were no time limits, no weight classes, no mandatory safety equipment and no judges. This meant that fights ended by knockout, submission or referee stoppage.

The time-limit dilemma reared its ugly head at the UFC 4 when the final match between Royce Gracie and Dan Severn went past the allotted pay-per-view time limit. As a result, TV viewers missed Gracie dramatically submitting Severn with a triangle choke to win the championship for a third time. Because of this mishap, SEG officials realized that they needed to institute time limits to prevent the same thing from happening again. So in 1995 at the UFC 5, they instituted a 30-minute time limit on all matches.

While this helped with the pay-per-view time constraints, another unsatisfying element occurred at the UFC 5. Because there were still no judges to determine a winner when the time limit expired, the much-anticipated rematch between Royce Gracie and Ken Shamrock ended in an unsatisfactory draw, which outraged fans. To resolve this problem, the second mishap resulted in SEG officials instituting judges at the UFC 6. However, even after the implementation of judges, the events had no established parameters on how to judge the fights and referees still couldn't stop fights. Early on, their job was to make sure that the few rules were enforced and to stop a bout only when a fighter submitted. Fortunately, the UFC gradually introduced more rules and regulations as time went along and gave referees the authority to stop fights.

Marketing the event as a blood sport also almost led to the sport's downfall. SEG officials boasted that it was a "no-holds-barred" fighting event in which anything could happen, even death. Initially, this was a successful marketing scheme to attract viewers, but it backfired as the political uproar drew increasing attention. In 1997, Sen. John McCain launched a campaign against the UFC, which he called "human cockfighting." McCain had enough influence that pay-per-view carriers began dropping the events from their lineups until the sport disappeared from U.S. television.

As a result, SEG faced bankruptcy. With its impending demise, SEG produced its last event, the UFC 29: *Defense of the Belts*, in 2000. During the dark period from 1997 to 2001, Canadian cable broadcasts, fan support on the Internet and live event attendance kept the sport alive.

The UFC remained a fringe sport on the verge of collapsing until Zuffa LLC—a Las Vegas-based media and casino management company owned by Lorenzo and Frank Fertitta—purchased it in 2001. ("Zuffa" is an Italian word meaning "to fight.") Being big fans of the sport, the Fertitta brothers planned to resurrect it and return it to its former popularity.

To legitimize the sport, they first sought to create sanctioned rules and regulations. The Fertitta brothers, along with their friend Dana White (appointed president of Zuffa LLC), succeeded in accomplishing this by soliciting support from the New Jersey State Athletic Control Board. Collectively, they drafted a new set of rules and regulations formally known as the Unified Rules of Mixed Martial Arts Combat. By establishing these new rules and regulations, they hoped to make the sport safer and change its image from a blood-sport spectacle to a respectable combat sport. The new rules featured five weight classes, rounds, time limits, 31 fouls and eight possible ways for fights to end. After its genesis, New Jersey was the first state to officially adopt the Unified Rules of Mixed Martial Arts Combat. Shortly thereafter, the highly sought-after state of Nevada followed suit and adopted New Jersey's unified rules on July 23, 2001. Many states, including California, Florida, and Louisiana subsequently adopted the rules, as well. This was a welcomed change that gave the UFC some much-needed support and credibility.

The new and improved Ultimate Fighting Championship resurfaced in 2001 with the UFC 30: *Battle on the Boardwalk*. The show returned with the pay-per-view ban lifted and sanctioning from the Nevada State Athletic Commission. With that, the event was heavily promoted and available to a much wider audience, who gave the sport a second chance. The show was considered a comeback success, and this started its resurgence as a combat sport to be reckoned with. Its acceptance as a "real" sport by the mainstream public would soon be coming.

Though the new UFC established a better image and was increasing in stature with each subsequent event, Zuffa was still not making the profit it desired. However, that all changed with the debut of the reality TV series *The Ultimate Fighter* on Spike TV. This show skyrocketed the UFC's mainstream popularity and increased its revenues, turning the UFC into a profitable venture for the Fertitta brothers and White.

The inaugural *TUF* show selected a group of 16 UFC fighter hopefuls vying for two exclusive contracts with the organization. The 16 fighters were divided into two teams of eight and separated into two weight divisions. The contestants were tasked to fight in single-elimination bouts, as matched up by the coaches and White. The show followed their trials and tribulations for eight weeks, yielding 12 episodes. Each episode featured the fighters interacting at the house that they shared, training sessions, and the fight between the two chosen fighters at the end of the episode. The series culminated with the four finalists fighting on the big season-finale show with the two winners each landing an exclusive six-figure contract. The show took the sport to another level of exposure and popularity because it marked the first time viewers could watch UFC fights on cable television for free.

The first season was a resounding success and was topped off by one of the greatest battles in UFC history. *The Ultimate Fighter* Season One light-heavyweight finals match between Forrest Griffin and Stephan Bonnar took place on April 9, 2005 and is considered to be the pivotal moment in the sport's history in terms of increasing mainstream acceptance. This is the fight that put the UFC on the map. It was a spectacular give-and-take, back-and-forth battle between two evenly matched, highly skilled combatants and ended with a stupendous finish. It was such a classic fight that White not only gave the winner Griffin an exclusive contract but also awarded the loser Bonnar with a contract for the effort both men exhibited. The first season was such a success that it has spawned eight seasons thus far.

While the sport continues to flourish largely because of the efforts of the Zuffa-owned UFC, there are other noteworthy North American-based organizations, such as Strikeforce, Affliction, Adrenaline and King of the Cage that have contributed to the sport's rise in recognition and popularity.

While it may appear to casual fans that the United States has a monopoly on MMA, it doesn't have the market cornered on the sport. Other prominent organizations exist that rival their American counterparts in popularity and importance in the sport's history and continuing evolution. The most significant ones have come from the Far East, specifically Japan. Japanese organizations such as Pancrase (which was actually the predecessor to the UFC by two months and has the distinction of being the first official MMA organization since the sport's re-emergence), Shooto, the defunct RINGS, the defunct K-1 Hero's, and most notably, the defunct PRIDE have done their share of popularizing the sport.

In March 2007, PRIDE lost their deal with Fuji Television because of alleged ties with the *yakuza* (Japanese mafia) and was bought by Zuffa to further solidify its status as the world's leading MMA promoter. However, in 2008, executives from the K-1 Hero's organization teamed up with former executives from PRIDE and established a new organization called Fighting Entertainment Group to once again rival the UFC. From the ashes of PRIDE and K-1 Hero's, FEG created the exceptional MMA promotion DREAM. Picking up where PRIDE left off, DREAM has established itself, alongside the UFC, as one of the premier MMA promoters in the world.

The other noteworthy MMA promotion which rivals both the UFC and PRIDE is World Victory Road from Japan. Like DREAM, this promotion was formed after the demise of PRIDE. This organization is significant in the MMA world because, along with signing several renown MMA fighters such as Takanori Gomi, Josh Barnett, Kevin Randleman and a host of others. They are the first MMA promotion to reach an agreement with Fuji TV since it dropped PRIDE in 2006. As such, it has the most widespread TV coverage in Japan. Moreover, WVR also reached a broadcast agreement with HDNET to televise their events in the United States.

Since its re-emergence in Brazil in 1925 via the Gracie family, MMA has truly expanded globally, with more and more local, regional and national events coming into fruition all over the world. With ever-increasing media coverage through the likes of ESPN, USA Today and other major media outlets in the United States, the sport continues its upward trajectory toward mainstream recognition and acceptance as a real combat sport. At the time of this writing, it currently holds the enviable position as the fastest-growing sport worldwide. For now and the foreseeable future, the outlook of the mixed martial arts appears bright and secure.

MIXED MARTIAL ARTS RULES

The rules that govern mixed-martial arts matches are fairly similar across the board with minor variations from country to country and organization to organization. While there are significant differences between two of the most prominent MMA organizations, what follows are the general rules common to most MMA organizations around the world, especially in the United States.

Weight Divisions

Most MMA organizations recognize and use the following five weight divisions:

Weight Division	Upper Limit in Pounds	Equivalent in Kilograms
Lightweight	155 lbs.	70 kgs.
Welterweight	170 lbs.	77 kgs.
Middleweight	185 lbs.	84 kgs.
Light Heavyweight	205 lbs.	93 kgs.
Heavyweight	265 lbs.	120 kgs.

The following weight divisions exist in a few MMA organizations, such as World Extreme Cagefighting:

Weight Division	Upper Limit in Pounds	Equivalent in Kilograms
Flyweight	125 lbs.	57 kgs.
Bantamweight	135 lbs.	61 kgs.
Featherweight	145 lbs.	66 kgs.

The super-heavyweight division (which has no upper-weight limit) is almost nonexistent these days.

Competition Attire/Apparel

Almost all MMA organizations have their competitors fight in approved shorts and do not allow shirts or shoes. The competitors must have their hands wrapped to prevent fractures and wear light but well-padded gloves that allow enough movement for grappling. The approved gloves must weigh between 4 ounces to 6 ounces (110 grams to 170 grams).

Bout Durations

Most MMA nonchampionship matches feature three five-minute rounds and give the fighters a one-minute rest in between rounds. Title fights are extended to five rounds.

Judging

Most MMA bouts are evaluated and scored by three judges using the 10-point must system as the standard method of scoring a bout. Under this system, each judge must award 10 points to the winner of the round and nine points or less to the loser, unless the two fighters tie the round, which is exceedingly rare.

Judges evaluate mixed-martial arts bouts based on the following criteria:

Effective Striking	The comparative total number of legal, meaningful heavy strikes landed by each fighter.
Effective Grappling	The number of successful legal takedowns, reversals and submission attempts along with who's able to maintain a more dominant position on the ground.
Ring Generalship	Who is dictating the action, the pace and the position of the bout. For example, when Fighter A thwarts a double-leg takedown from Fighter B with a sprawl and follows it up with a barrage of strikes, Fighter A is controlling the fight, thus commanding ring generalship.
Effective Aggressiveness	The fighter who exerts constant forward pressure and effectively attacks his opponent, landing legal, potent strikes.
Effective Defense	The fighter who most effectively avoids being struck, taken down or reversed while effectively countering to regain the initiative.

Scoring Criteria

The following objective scoring criteria is what MMA judges use when scoring a round:

1. A round is scored 10-10 by the judges when both fighters appear to be fighting evenly and neither contestant shows clear dominance in a round.

2. A round is scored 10-9 by the judges when a fighter wins it by a close margin, landing the greater number of effective legal strikes, takedowns and reversals along with attempting more submissions.

3. A round is scored 10-8 by the judges when a fighter overwhelmingly dominates his opponent by knocking him down with a strike or almost submitting him.

4. A round is scored 10-7 by the judges when a fighter totally dominates his opponent by completely out-striking (staggering and/or knocking him down one or more times) and/or out-grappling him (multiple submission attempts that were almost successful).

MMA judges look at effective striking, effective grappling, ring generalship, effective aggressiveness and effective defense on a sliding scale to objectively score a bout, taking into account the length of time one fighter dominates the other in all phases of an MMA fight. The sliding scale goes like this:

1. If the fighters spend most of a round on the ground, then effective grappling is weighed first followed by effective striking.

2. If the fighters spend most of a round in a stand-up position, then effective striking is weighed first followed by effective grappling.

3. If a round finishes with a relatively even amount of stand-up and ground fighting, then effective striking and effective grappling are weighed equally.

Ways to Win

Because MMA encompasses ground fighting, there are nine ways to win a mixed-martial arts match instead of eight like in boxing and kickboxing:

1. Knockout (KO): When a fighter is rendered unconscious because of strikes (punches, kicks, knees or elbows) or by chokes (rear-naked choke, guillotine, triangle, etc), his opponent is declared the winner. Because MMA rules allow ground fighting, a fight is immediately stopped to prevent the unconscious fighter from taking more blows and sustaining further injury.

2. Submission: A fighter can win by performing a grappling technique that causes his opponent to surrender, renders his opponent unconscious or forces the referee to stop the fight. A fighter surrenders by tapping on an opponent's body, tapping on the mat or by verbal declaration.

3. Technical Knockout (TKO): The referee has the authority to stop a match at any time if a fighter is dominating his opponent to such an extent that he is unable to intelligently defend himself from further attacks. This includes the opponent appearing to be semiconscious from strikes, made unconscious from a chokehold, or appears to have sustained a significant injury such as a broken bone.

4. **Doctor Stoppage:** A referee can call a timeout to determine whether a competitor can continue fighting competently or if his injuries—such as a severely lacerated forehand—are too severe. Once the referee separates the fighters, the designated ring doctor inspects the fighter. If he decides that the competitor cannot continue fighting, the fight ends and his opponent is declared the victor. However, if a match is stopped as a result of an illegal action by the opponent, either his opponent will be disqualified or a no contest will be declared.

5. **Corner Stoppage:** A fighter's cornermen may concede defeat on a fighter's behalf by throwing in the towel while the match is in progress or in between rounds.

6. **Decision:** If a match goes the distance, three predesignated judges—whose score cards are tallied after the fight is over—determine the outcome of the bout. Once a fight goes to decision, there are four possible outcomes. 1. A unanimous decision means that all three judges scored the fight in favor of the same fighter. 2. A split decision means that two out of the three judges scored the fight for the same fighter. 3. A majority decision means two judges declared one fighter the winner, while the other one declared the fight a draw. 4.

MMA IN JAPAN

Based on how the sport evolved across the Pacific, Japanese MMA promotions differ from the American counterparts in several key ways. Here are the major differences between the **Ultimate Fighting Championship** and **DREAM**, Japan's biggest MMA promoter:

DREAM matches take place in a ring, while **UFC** bouts take place in a cage.

DREAM allows knee strikes to the head along with soccer kicks and foot stomps to the body of a grounded/downed opponent. It also allows a grounded/downed fighter to execute up-kicks to the head. The **UFC** doesn't allow these things.

The **UFC** allows elbow strikes but **DREAM** doesn't.

Standard **UFC** matches last for three five-minute rounds (title fights last five rounds) with one-minute rest periods in between. **DREAM** conducts matches consisting of a 10-minute first round followed by a five-minute second round with 90-second rest periods in between.

The **UFC** scores fights using the 10-point must system for each round, while **DREAM** scores fights in their entirety.

The **UFC** allows for draws in its decisions, while **DREAM** judges must pick a winner.

A draw means that the fight was scored as a tie between the two fighters in one of three ways—a unanimous draw (all three judges scored the fight a draw), a majority draw (two of the three judges scored the fight a draw, while one declared a clear victor) and a split draw (one judge scored the fight for one fighter, another judge scored the fight for the other fighter and the third judge scored the fight a draw).

7. Forfeit: A fighter or one of his representatives may forfeit a match before the beginning of the match, thereby losing the match by default.

8. Disqualification: The referee might warn a fighter who performs a foul, illegal action, or does not follow the referee's instructions by committing the following infractions: holding or grabbing the fence, holding an opponent's shorts or gloves, or the presence of a corner-man on the fighting-area perimeter for more than one second. After the first warning, if the prohibited conduct persists, a penalty, often in the form of a deduction of points, may be issued before disqualification. Generally, if a fighter receives three warnings, he will be disqualified. A fighter will also be disqualified if his opponent is injured and unable to continue because of a deliberately executed illegal technique on his part.

9. No Contest: When both fighters commit a violation of the rules or one fighter is unable to continue because of an injury that incurred from an accidentally executed illegal technique, the match is declared a "no contest."

Note: The referee may restart the action if the fighters reach a stalemate and do not work to improve position or finish.

Fouls

There are numerous techniques and actions that are fouls in MMA. The following list delineates them:

1. Head butting (a move in which a fighter uses his head as a weapon to strike an opponent)

2. Eye gouging

3. Biting

4. Hair pulling

5. Fish-hooking (putting a finger into an orifice of an opponent—usually the mouth—and pulling with the intent of offensively manipulating an opponent's position by causing injury to that orifice in the process)

6. Groin attacks

7. Putting a finger into any orifice or into any cut or laceration on an opponent

8. Small joint manipulation (any hold that twists, pops or hyperextends a small joint, such as the fingers or toes)

9. Striking to the back of the head or neck (otherwise known as rabbit punching)

10. Striking downward on any part of an opponent's body using the point of the elbow

11. Throat strikes of any kind, including grabbing the trachea

12. Clawing, pinching or twisting the flesh

13. Grabbing the clavicle

14. Kicking or kneeing the head of a downed opponent

15. Stomping any part of the body of a downed opponent

16. Kicking to the kidney with the heels

17. Slamming/spiking an opponent to the canvas on his head or neck

18. Throwing an opponent out of a ring or cage

19. Grabbing or putting a hand inside the shorts or gloves of an opponent

20. Spitting at an opponent

21. Engaging in unsportsmanlike conduct that causes an injury to an opponent

22. Purposely holding the cage fence or the ring ropes

23. Using abusive language in the ring or cage

24. Attacking an opponent on or during the break

25. Attacking an opponent who is under the care of the referee

26. Attacking an opponent after the bell has sounded at the end of a round

27. Blatantly and flagrantly disregarding the instructions of the referee

28. Timidity (avoiding engagement with an opponent or intentionally or consistently dropping the mouthpiece or faking an injury)

29. Interference by the corner

30. Throwing in the towel during competition

31. Running out of the cage or ring

Now you know the general rules for MMA fights. From here on out is the reference guide. Enjoy!

THE REFERENCE GUIDE

The mixed-martial arts reference guide is structured like a dictionary. Each entry contains a clear description, common applications and entertaining facts. There are also appendix and reference sections on the sport and its integral components. Like a dictionary, it starts with the A's and works its way to the Z's.

I've broken entries into three main categories. The "Description" is a brief rundown about the technique or term. The "Applications" are detailed examples of the technique in action. The "Insights" offer fun supplemental info on the technique.

At the end of the book, before the index, there is a glossary of common terms not included in the reference guide.

AMERICANA

Description

The Americana is a submission hold that traps the wrist and cranks the shoulder in a figure-4 hold. It is usually executed from the mount or side-control position. What distinguishes it from the *kimura* is its upward rather than downward L-shape.

Applications
Americana From the Mount

1-3. After grounding-and-pounding his adversary, Fighter A pins down the opponent's left arm.

4. Fighter A traps the opponent's left wrist and arm to the ground with both hands. Notice how Fighter B's arm is in a palm-up L-shape position.

5. Sliding his right hand underneath Fighter B's left upper arm, Fighter A executes a figure-4 wrist hold.

6. If the hold is secure, Fighter A immediately raises his right forearm while simultaneously sliding his left wrist and the opponent's arm toward their hips. This cranks Fighter B's shoulder, forcing him to tap in submission to avoid having his shoulder dislocated.

Insights

- A fighter can make his hold more secure if he posts or places his forehead on the ground while cranking the shoulder. Doing so gives him a stronger base, making him more stable.

- No matter how he executes the hold, the fighter needs to keep the opponent's arm bent at a 90-degree angle to secure the lock properly. If the fighter doesn't, the opponent can counter the hold by bending his arm toward his own head or stretching his arm out. The 90-degree angle also helps apply the most torque.

- To firmly secure the hold, a competitor presses his elbow tightly against his adversary's head, close to the jaw line. This acts like a wedge. It makes it difficult for the opponent to pull or push his arm out of the figure-4 hold.

Americana From Side Control

1-2. From his dominant side-control position, Fighter A distracts his adversary with elbow strikes before transitioning into an Americana.

3. In this example, he pins Fighter B's wrist with one hand, creating the palm-up L-shape position.

4. Once his opponent is pinned, Fighter A executes the figure-4 hold.

5. From this point, Fighter A lifts his right forearm while simultaneously sliding his and his rival's left wrists toward Fighter B's hip. This will tear Fighter B's shoulder unless he taps out.

Additional Information
- ☞ figure-4 hold
- ☞ kimura

ANACONDA CHOKE

Description

The anaconda choke is a submission hold that can render an opponent unconscious by restricting blood flow to the brain. This occurs when the choke constricts the carotid arteries in the neck, which cuts off blood flow to the brain. For the technique to be considered an anaconda choke, the combatants must be facedown in the north/south position and the defending fighter's arm must be trapped and pressing into his own neck.

Application
General Anaconda Choke Scenario

1-3. Fighter A thwarts a double-leg takedown with a sprawl.

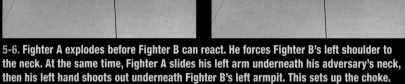

4. Fighter A immediately pushes Fighter B's head down to the ground with his right hand while bringing his knees in closer to his opponent's head.

5-6. Fighter A explodes before Fighter B can react. He forces Fighter B's left shoulder to the neck. At the same time, Fighter A slides his left arm underneath his adversary's neck, then his left hand shoots out underneath Fighter B's left armpit. This sets up the choke.

7. As soon as Fighter A's arm-triangle position is tightly locked, the anaconda choke is executed.

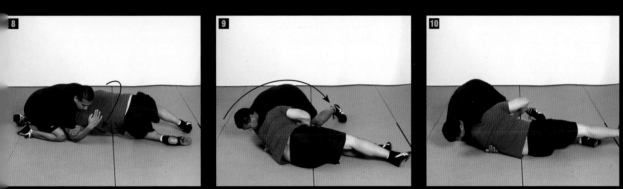

8-10. To tighten his hold and submit his opponent, he twists Fighter B's arms and upper body clockwise. This rolls Fighter B onto his left side. While turning his opponent, Fighter A squeezes his arms together and simultaneously moves his own body like the hand of a clock. By shifting his feet closer to his opponent's body while maintaining the lock, Fighter A increases pressure on the neck.

11. If Fighter B doesn't submit, he will be rendered unconscious.

Additional Information
- ☞ D'Arce choke
- ☞ guillotine choke
- ☞ north/south position
- ☞ rear-naked choke
- ☞ sprawl

ANKLE LOCK

Description

These submission holds are also known as Achilles locks for the Greek warrior with the famously weak ankles. A competitor executes the locks with a hand-to-wrist grip or figure-4 hold. He then squeezes the ankle with his grip while simultaneously thrusting his hips—both of which hyperextend his opponent's ankle, causing immense pain. If the opponent doesn't submit, the ankle will break. Note: The thrust isn't demonstrative, instead it is a slight arch that supplements the lock.

Application
Ankle Lock (Front and Side View)

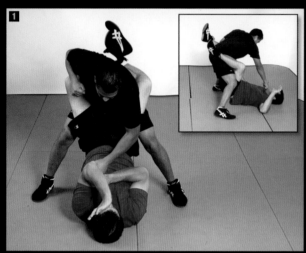

1. In a standing position from inside the opponent's closed guard, Fighter A grounds-and-pounds Fighter B until his legs open.

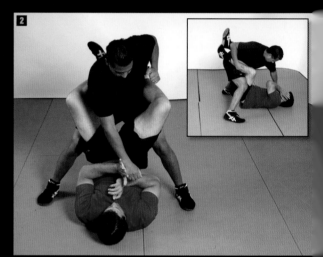

2. With the guard open, Fighter A prepares to transition into an ankle lock.

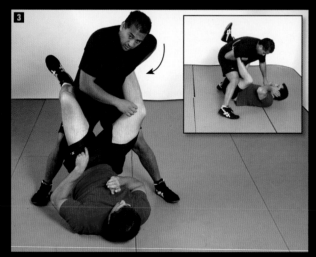

3. To trap his adversary, Fighter A hooks his left arm around Fighter B's ankle.

4. While he does this, Fighter A drops to the ground with the opponent's right leg trapped in between his legs. Depending on the situation, he sometimes secures his hold with two hands.

Insights

- If the fighter doesn't securely lock the ankle with his arm, tightly squeeze his legs together and apply pressure on the thigh/groin area with his foot, his arch might be nullified, allowing the opponent to turn into the lock and escape.

- In order for this technique to work effectively, it must be secured and executed rapidly. The longer it takes a fighter to execute the lock, as with all submission holds, the greater the likelihood of a counter.

- Securing the hold by squeezing the legs works better than squeezing the arms because the legs are much stronger.

- In the examples, the ankle lock from the front view is technically called a "foot-down inside right" ankle lock. The ankle lock from the side view is called a "foot-down inside left." They are "foot-down" and "inside" because the fighter executes the technique with the rival's foot underneath his body and inside because it is held next to the fighter's side that is against the floor. Ankle locks can also be performed in a "foot-up" outside (above your body) position. The inside ankle lock is the more secure and effective of the two variations, however.

- In regards to the figure-4 hold or hand-on-wrist hold, there is no difference in effectiveness. It just depends on the fighter's personal preference.

- Being on his side grants a fighter more leverage because he is able to arch his back more freely. As a result, a competitor is more likely to hyperextend his opponent's ankles when he's in this position.

- A typical counter against the ankle lock is to sit up to prevent the antagonist from applying pressure to the ankle. He does this by grabbing on the attacking fighter's elbow or arm, which allows him to pull himself up into a seated position.

5. While both competitors are on the ground, Fighter A immediately executes a figure-4 hold by placing his unhooked hand on Fighter B's shin and gripping it with his hooked hand.

6. From this position, Fighter B is almost trapped. To submit him, Fighter A squeezes his legs together with his top foot pressing against his opponent's inner thigh or groin area. He finishes by arching or thrusting his hips forward to hyperextend the ankle.

Additional Information
- ☞ closed guard
- ☞ figure-4 holds
- ☞ open guard

ARMBAR

Description

An armbar traps an opponent's elbow between the fighter's legs in a cross-body position with the corresponding wrist secured by the fighter's hands. It becomes a submission hold when the fighter thrusts his hips upward against the immobilized elbow joint. Two other names for the armbar are the "cross-body armbar" because of the cross-body position and a "straight armbar" because of the positioning of the opponent's arm in the lock.

Applications
Armbar Executed From Inside the Closed Guard

1. From inside the closed guard, Fighter A traps Fighter B's arm with both hands and pins it to his chest for greater control.

2. Once the arm is secured, he immediately places his left foot on his adversary's right hip to maneuver his own hips counter-clockwise. Fighter A also presses his left hand to the side of Fighter B's face while sliding his right leg under Fighter B's armpit. This helps Fighter A turn his hips and clear Fighter B's head so he can perform the armbar.

3. As the competitors move into perpendicular positions, Fighter A swings his left leg around and over Fighter B's exposed head.

4. He also transitions his hands so his left controls Fighter B's right wrist and his right controls Fighter B's right forearm.

5. With the arm trapped, Fighter B is forced into a supine position. To do this, Fighter A pushes with his legs and pulls on his adversary's arm to straighten it, giving Fighter A better leverage.

6. Once his adversary is prone, Fighter A "glues" Fighter B's arm to his chest, squeezes his knees together, and explosively thrusts his hips up against Fighter B's elbow for a submission. If Fighter B doesn't tap, his arm will break.

Insights

- This is a fundamental, bread-and-butter submission hold in MMA. It is very versatile because it can be effectively executed from all the major ground positions, such as the guard, mount, back control and side control. An opponent can be submitted by it in a prone or supine position, faceup or facedown.

- For the best leverage, a fighter maneuvers his opponent's elbow over his hip and pins his opponent's hand against his chest with his thumb up and his pinky down, glued to his chest. See photo 5 below.

- The legs do most of the work in applying pressure on the elbow.

- This was one of Royce Gracie and Frank Shamrock's favorite techniques in the early days of the sport.

Armbar Executed From a Back-Control Position

1. From a back-control position, Fighter A transitions into the armbar by using his right leg to push against his opponent's thigh and maneuver himself into a perpendicular position.

2. He also pushes against Fighter B's face and rib cage to obtain the cross-body position.

3. Once he's set up, Fighter A immediately swings his left leg over and on top of Fighter B's head while transitioning his hands into a better, more secure trap position.

4. In the process, Fighter A drives his opponent flat on the ground by pushing with his legs and pulling at the trapped arm, straightening it out for better leverage.

5. When Fighter B is grounded, Fighter A squeezes his knees together and thrusts his hips upward to submit his adversary.

Additional Information
☞ back control
☞ closed guard
☞ open guard

ARM DRAG

Description

The arm drag is a transitional move used to maneuver a fighter from a front position to a side or rear one. It is a fundamental wrestling technique that starts from a neutral wrestling tie-up position, like the clinch.

Application
Arm Drag to Rear-Body Lock

1. From a wrestling tie-up position, Fighter A plans to execute an arm drag in order to move from a front position to a rear-control position.

2. Acting on the element of surprise, Fighter A grasps the underside of Fighter B's upper arm and jerks it downward suddenly. This moves his adversary out of the neutral tie-up position.

Insights

- This is one of amateur wrestling's basic moves. It was a technique more prevalently and successfully used in the early days of MMA. It's not as successfully employed these days because the level of clinch fighting has evolved to a higher skill set.

- Because of the preponderance of collegiate wrestlers in the MMA ranks, the arm drag is still an important skill for non-wrestlers to master to keep it from being used against them.

3. Simultaneously, Fighter A takes two steps to get behind his opponent.

4. Once there, Fighter A executes a rear-body lock from which he can take his opponent down in a variety of ways or return to a stand-up fighting position.

Additional Information
☞ dirty boxing clinch
☞ muay Thai clinch
☞ wrestling clinch

ARM TRIANGLE

Description

The arm triangle is a blood-choke technique in which the fighter encircles his opponent's neck and arm in a figure-4 hold. This causes the opponent to be rendered unconscious or submit. The choke restricts blood flow via compression of the adversary's carotid arteries.

Application
Transition From the Mount

1. In the mount position, Fighter A grounds-and-pounds his opponent.

2. He transitions into the arm triangle by targeting one of Fighter B's arms. In this case, Fighter A plans to target the left arm.

3. Diving in for the choke, Fighter A wraps his left arm around Fighter B's head. Simultaneously, he pushes Fighter B's left arm to the right then uses the left side of his head and neck to trap Fighter B's left arm.

4. Going chest-to-chest and head-to-head, Fighter A secures the triangle choke.

Insights

- "Based out" is a common term used to describe how a fighter spreads his legs to improve his stability and leverage.

- Besides having a tight arm wrapped around the opponent's head, it's important for a fighter to bury and press his head against his opponent's to fully constrict him. Doing so prevents the opponent from using his trapped left arm to counter the choke.

- Technically, the choke is a stranglehold because it constricts the carotid arteries rather than the windpipe. "Choke" or "blood choke" is just the more commonly applied term in MMA.

Additional Information
- ☞ anaconda choke
- ☞ D'Arce choke
- ☞ side control

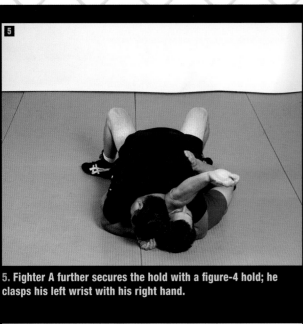

5. Fighter A further secures the hold with a figure-4 hold; he clasps his left wrist with his right hand.

6. To execute the choke, Fighter A then transitions into a side-control position by lifting and moving his left leg.

7. With his legs "based out" to stabilize his control position, Fighter A buries his head against his opponent's head and squeezes his arms together.

8. This causes Fighter B to tap out or be rendered unconscious by the restriction of blood to his brain.

ARM WRAP

Description

A mounted fighter can reposition an opponent to his side with an arm wrap. The technique is characterized by a wrap—the mounted fighter traps and wraps one of the rival's arms around the rival's head while rolling him to the side. During the technique, the opponent is completely immobilized and unable to strike back at his attacker. A fighter uses the arm wrap to transition to a new position where he can obtain back control, ground-and-pound his opponent or execute various submission holds.

Application
Arm Wrap Reposition to Side Mount

1. From the mount position, Fighter A punches the opponent's face to "soften" him up and make him extend his arms to block the attack.

2. The extension makes Fighter B vulnerable because Fighter A can now execute an arm wrap. He drives his left arm across Fighter B's face.

3. While he does this, Fighter A drops his chest on top of Fighter B's left arm, pinning the arm against his rival's chest.

4. To wrap his opponent's arm, Fighter A slides his right hand underneath Fighter B's neck. This allows him to grip Fighter B's wrist. Fighter A then transitions his hold on Fighter B's wrist by switching from a left grip to a right grip.

5. Continuing the arm wrap, Fighter A begins to rise, capping Fighter B's elbow with his left hand. Like a steering wheel, Fighter A will push with his left hand and pull with his right to roll Fighter B over.

6. Fighter A also posts his left foot—with toes pointing outward and the heel presse against his belly— and positions his right knee against Fighter B's upper back. This gives him the leverage to roll his opponen because even though Fighter B can't move he's not so constricted that he can't roll.

Insights

- The arm wrap is a good position to control an opponent and ground-and-pound him. However, a fighter has a hard time obtaining it because the opponent will try not to extend his arms. It leaves them vulnerable to armbars and other submission holds.

- Another reason why the arm wrap is so potent is because the mounted fighter moves to a position where the opponent can't see him, can't strike him and can't protect himself from hand and elbow strikes.

- When performing the arm wrap, it's important not only to pin the arm but also to lock the wrist. If a fighter doesn't lock it, then the opponent can still escape.

- When sliding his hand under his opponent's head, a fighter will keep his palm down because it facilitates the movement.

- In the illustration, Fighter A reaches his "posted" position by taking "baby steps" (heel to toe) with his left leg. This also allows Fighter A to open up a little bit so he can roll Fighter B to the side.

7. Now that he's in a side-mount position, Fighter A grounds-and-pounds Fighter B with punches and elbow strikes to the head.

8-10. Fighter A can also finish his adversary by transitioning into a submission hold like the armbar.

Additional Information
☞ armbar

BACK CONTROL

Description

A fighter is in back control, a fundamental grappling position, when his opponent's back is facing the fighter's chest. This is a very advantageous position to obtain because the opponent can't see, strike at or defend against the attacker; he's at the fighter's mercy. However, back control is not a submission hold; instead, it is a position from which to transition and perform other techniques or strikes. Competitors can execute back control from any position, regardless of whether the opponent is prone, supine, seated or turtled. A fighter can further secure his position by using grapevines or underhooks. If the opponent is prone, the position can also be referred to as a "back mount."

Applications
Back Control With Grapevines

1. Fighter A obtains a back-mount position on his prone opponent.

2. Fighter A secures his back-control position by inserting his feet underneath Fighter B's inner thighs and hooking them with his heels (grapevining).

3. To put and keep his adversary "flat on the deck" or prone, Fighter A then thrusts his hips forward and down, extending Fighter B's hips and causing Fighter B's legs to rise.

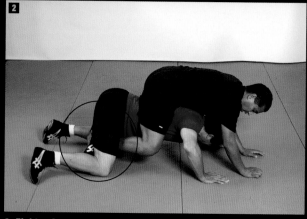

4. From this position, Fighter A can ground-and-pound Fighter B's head. He could also apply a rear-naked choke to submit him.

Insights

- Because the opponent is so helpless, back control is the ideal position from which to apply a rear-naked choke or transition into a host of other submission holds, such as armbars and triangles. The rear-naked choke is the most prevalent submission hold applied from back control.

- Back control means that a fighter is directly behind his opponent. In the case of the back mount, Fighter A just needs to be sitting on Fighter B to achieve the position. However, a fighter doesn't want to just sit there. If anything, he wants to pound on his opponent—the most secure way of doing so is by striking the head. Note: MMA rules dictate that a competitor can only strike the side of the head; he cannot strike the back of the head or neck.

- The body triangle is also a form of back control and is becoming more common.

Back Control With Grapevines and Underhooks

1. Fighter A has back control on an opponent who is trying to stand up.

2-3. However, Fighter A is able to stick to Fighter B like a leach, even as he rolls onto his back.

4. Once in a supine position, Fighter A transitions into a rear-naked choke to submit Fighter B.

Back Control From Supine Position

This photo shows back control when the opponent is in a supine position (on top).

Additional Information
- ☞ grapevine
- ☞ body triangle
- ☞ turtle position
- ☞ underhooks

BODY-LOCK TAKEDOWNS

Description

Body-lock takedowns are the most basic and primal way to take someone to the ground. The technique has two main characteristics: a bear-hug hold and a takedown. A fighter secures his opponent's torso via a bear hug that traps none, one or both of the rival's arm. Then, he can take down his adversary through a variety of ways, such as a pickup and slam, outside trip or inside trip.

Applications
Body-Lock Takedown With Pickup and Slam

1-2. While squaring off, Fighter A shoots a left cross, right jab combination to distract his opponent. By doing this, Fighter B is unable to concentrate on takedown defense, allowing Fighter A to bridge the gap.

3. Fighter A penetrates the gap by stepping deeply toward Fighter B.

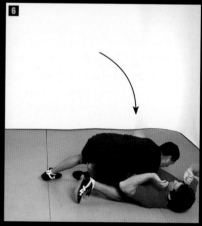

4. Fighter A secures a body lock by bear-hugging Fighter B around the lower torso. He also presses his hips against Fighter B's hips in order to lift him off the ground. This gives Fighter A leverage.

5. Using his legs, Fighter A picks up Fighter B.

6. He slams him to the ground, immediately securing side-control position.

Insights

- Takedowns aren't about pure strength. Instead, the key element, besides a tight bear hug, is for a fighter to press his hips against the opponent's hips, constricting his rival and preventing an escape. There's a saying in Brazilian *jiu-jitsu*: "Contact equals control, and space equals escape." The farther away the fighter's hips are from each other, the less control and leverage he has in securing his takedown.

- With that in mind, creating space is the most obvious counter to a body-lock takedown. Space allows an opponent to sprawl or execute other escapes.

Body Lock Takedown With Outside Trip

1. Fighter A secures a body-lock takedown by bear-hugging Fighter B's waist.

2-3. Instead of lifting him up for a slam, Fighter A uses an outside trip to take him to the ground.

4. Once grounded, he secures a side-control position where he can ground-and-pound his opponent or go for a submission.

Additional Information
☞ double-leg takedown
☞ ground and pound
☞ sprawl

BODY TRIANGLE

Description

A body triangle constricts the torso of an opponent with a leg figure-4 hold. It's disconcerting because it's very difficult to break. In theory, a fighter could hold his opponents in a body triangle indefinitely, but generally, it is used by a fighter to actively secure back control and/or transition into a submission like the rear-naked choke. A fighter executes a body triangle when he locks his legs in a figure-4 hold around his opponent's torso.

Applications
General Scenario for a Body Triangle

Fighter A has back control and secures it with a body triangle. He wraps his legs around Fighter B's torso, locking the triangle by placing his right leg over his left foot. This secures Fighter A's left foot underneath the crook of his right knee. From this position, Fighter A squeezes the figure-4 hold to put tremendous pressure on Fighter B's midsection.

Insights

- Because the body triangle is a form of back control, the opponent is basically at the mercy of his attacker. He can't turn to face or strike at the fighter. The only possible counter to a body triangle is for the opponent to twist and turn to face the competitor in back control, but that is extremely difficult to accomplish.

- How well the move works depends on the length of a fighter's legs in comparison to his opponent's girth. If the fighter has short legs and his opponent has a thick torso, the move won't be as effective.

- Generally, a body triangle is used to maintain back control or transition into a submission hold. However, it is possible to squeeze an opponent into submission, especially if the fighter has long, strong legs.

- As mentioned earlier, a fighter could indefinitely hold his adversary in a body triangle. Usually, it's common to see a fighter fight for a certain submission hold or transition into something else to move along the action of a fight.

Leg Positioning for the Body Triangle

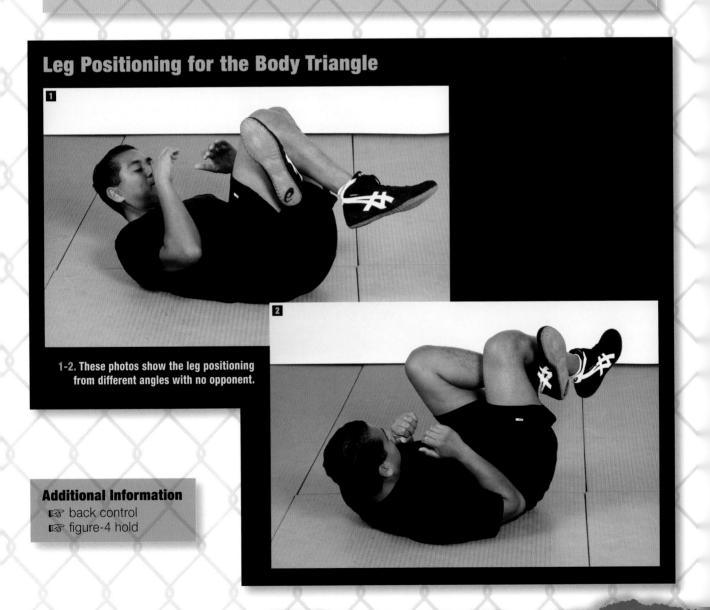

1-2. These photos show the leg positioning from different angles with no opponent.

Additional Information
☞ back control
☞ figure-4 hold

BRIDGING ESCAPE

Description

Because being mounted is considered the second-worst position in MMA, a bridging escape allows a fighter on the bottom to reverse his position with the opponent on top. For it to work, the opponent must be sitting over the fighter's hips with an arm and leg trapped to one side. This allows the fighter on the bottom to maneuver a mounted adversary around his own hips by thrusting them upward. This off-balances the opponent, so the fighter can roll and reverse positions.

Application
Bridging Escape to Mount

1. While Fighter B rains down punches from the mount position, Fighter A prepares to bridge an escape by parrying and using his elbows to scoot Fighter B down, over his hips.

2-3. Once Fighter B is over his hips, Fighter A explosively thrusts his hips upward, causing his opponent to lose balance and fall forward.

4-5. As soon as his opponent places his hands on the ground to steady himself, Fighter A immediately traps Fighter B's right arm by overhooking it.

Insights

- This is one of the fundamental maneuvers to off-balance and get an opponent out of a mounted position.

- If the bottom fighter is in a back-mount position, he can't escape because he can't bridge his hips in this position.

- In the illustrated example, Fighter A "scoots" Fighter B over his hips. A mounted antagonist ideally wants to sit on his opponent's chest. This secures his position and nullifies any attempts for the opponent to buck him off. Fighter A's elbows act as wedges to stop Fighter B from moving forward.

- A fighter doesn't have to bear-hug an opponent's torso. He can also just drive his free arm up and over the adversary's body, using the momentum to roll him over.

- Oftentimes, it takes more than one "buck" to displace an opponent, so a fighter shouldn't give up after one try.

- In Brazilian *jiu-jitsu*, this move is informally known as an *upa*.

6. While trapping the adversary's arm tightly against his side, Fighter A traps Fighter B's right foot by placing his left foot over it. Simultaneously, Fighter A places his right hand on his left hip (Note: This is not shown.)

7. With the opponent's arm and foot trapped, Fighter A places his right hand on his opponent's hip to augment the roll's momentum while arching.

8. Fighter B is now supine and Fighter A is now in the mount; their positions are reversed. Fighter A immediately immobilizes Fighter B's arms with biceps control, placing both hands on the corresponding biceps. From here, Fighter A can begin grounding-and-pounding, pass the guard or transition into another position.

Additional Information

- ☞ back control
- ☞ covering
- ☞ mount
- ☞ passing the guard

BUTTERFLY GUARD

Description

The butterfly guard is an open-guard position in which the insteps of a fighter's feet are hooked underneath the opponent's inner thighs. This helps a competitor maintain the gap between him and his top-positioned opponent and thwart any strikes or efforts the opponent makes to pass the guard. From the butterfly guard, an opponent can also go on the offensive with reversals and sweeps from this position.

Applications
Butterfly Guard (Side View)

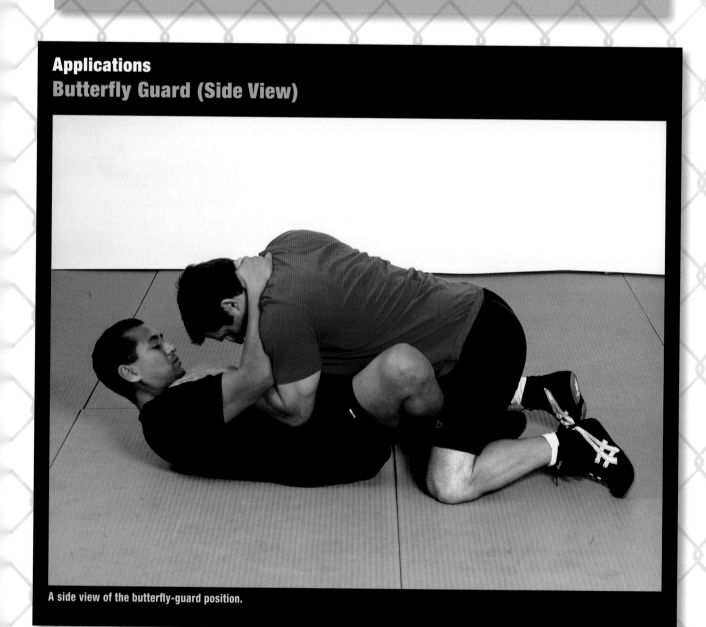

A side view of the butterfly-guard position.

Insights

- This is a very good position for a fighter to reverse someone from his guard. It allows the fighter to knock his opponent off-balance and manipulate his body weight to create the leverage to reverse him without too much effort.

- The butterfly guard is not to be confused with the half-butterfly, which isn't a defensive guard but a transition to facilitate a sweep.

Butterfly Guard (Front View)

A front backside view of the butterfly-guard position. Note how Fighter A's feet are hooked underneath Fighter B's inner thighs.

Additional Information

- 🖙 half-butterfly elevator sweep
- 🖙 open guard
- 🖙 passing the guard

CAN-OPENER

Description

Much like an actual can opener, the purpose of the can-opener technique is to free a fighter trapped in the closed-guard position. The fighter secures a two-handed hold around the back of his opponent's neck and puts pressure on it by cranking the head forward. This constricts the opponent's spine so much that the only way he can relieve it is by opening up his legs and the guard.

Application
General Scenario to Break the Closed Guard

1-2. After distracting his opponent with a punch, Fighter A gets his hands around the back of Fighter B's neck.

3. Fighter A obtains a two-handed hold around Fighter B's head. Note: He overlaps his hands rather than interlaces them.

4. From this position, Fighter A pulls Fighter B's head toward his stomach. He also arches his hips forward while simultaneously exerting pressure against Fighter B's neck with his arms.

Insights

- A common can-opener counter is to simply push the opponent's forearms out at his wrists.

- Even though a fighter breaks the closed guard, he still has to do something to change his position. The can opener allows him the space and freedom to obtain a more dominant position, execute an escape, pass the guard, etc.

- Cranking the head puts a lot of pressure on an opponent's spine. The technique curls the opponent into a ball, forcing him to open his legs to relieve pressure.

- While more common in the early days of MMA, the newer breed of fighters are more likely to ground and pound free of the closed-guard position.

5. This pain forces Fighter B to open his legs to alleviate the pain.

6. Fighter A can now escape or pass the guard into a better position, such as side control.

Additional Information
☞ half-butterfly elevator sweep
☞ passing the guard

CLOSED GUARD

Description

The closed guard is a fundamental defensive position in which a supine fighter traps his adversary between his legs. He wraps his legs around the opponent's torso and secures the position by crossing his ankles. From the closed guard, a competitor controls a top-positioned opponent by using his own hip and leg muscles to pull the opponent in and push him away. In conjunction with the hold, a fighter can also use his hands and arms to strike, grab, block, parry and pull in the opponent.

Application
Closed Guard With Pull-In Defense

1. Fighter A is on the bottom in a closed-guard position and vulnerable to Fighter B's strikes.

2. Because he has the better position, Fighter B is able to throw a right hook at Fighter A.

3. Fighter A's closed guard still gives him some control over the situation. He blocks the strike.

4. Using his legs, Fighter A pulls in his opponent. He also wraps his right arm around Fighter B's neck and overhooks Fighter B's right arm with his left arm.

Insights

- When people say "guard," they mean the closed guard.

- In a defensive bottom position, the closed guard is the "best" bad position to be in because a fighter can still manipulate his opponent and transition into submissions, sweeps, reversals and escapes. This happens in the illustration when Fighter A takes away the space between him and his opponent. He obtains even more control over Fighter B and makes it more difficult for his adversary to strike, break free or readopt his seated—or worse, standing—upright position.

- Sometimes, people think of the closed guard as a "neutral position" because either fighter can still go on the attack.

- Because the legs are wrapped around the opponent's torso, that makes them the best body part to move and control an opponent in this position. That's why the legs are primarily used for offense and the arms are used for defense in the closed-guard position.

5. Tightly holding Fighter B's body to his own upper body, Fighter A secures his position.

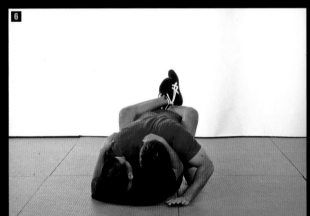

6. From here, Fighter A can effectively channel his efforts into escaping, reversing or transitioning into a number of submission holds like an armbar, triangle choke, kimura or back control into a rear-naked choke.

Additional Information
☞ armbar
☞ back control
☞ kimura
☞ rear-naked choke
☞ triangle choke

Description

Covering acts like a shield between a fighter and his attacking opponent. It is defined as action in which the arms and legs are used to block an opponent's strikes—punches, kicks, elbows or knees—from hitting vulnerable targets, like the head or ribs.

Applications
Covering the Left Hook (Front and Rear View)

1-2. Fighter A uses a right-arm cover against his opponent's lead left hook to the head. To effectively cover a hook, Fighter A tucks his chin and raises his arms, which are tightly bent at the elbows to form a triangular shape. His right hand covers the right side of his head to shield it from the hook.

Insights

- In the pictures illustrating a side cover against a hook punch, the fighter's left hand is up, covering the other side of his head. This is always a good thing to do because it protects the other side of a combatant's head from a follow-up shot by the opponent.

- When blocking a high round kick to the head, it is a safer to block it by using both arms instead of one. Using one arm can damage one or both forearm bones (ulna and radius), such as when Cung Le's kick broke Frank Shamrock's forearm in a Strikeforce event in March 2008.

- If a fighter decides to use a one-arm block against a high round kick, he should keep his arm pressed against the side of his head to absorb some of the force like a shock absorber.

Covering the Right Round Kick (Front and Rear View)

1-2. To block the adversary's right round kick to the head, Fighter A uses a two-arm cover. He raises his arms together, parallel to each other and perpendicular to the ground.

Additional Information
☞ parrying
☞ round kick

CROSS (PUNCH)

Description

This is one of the core bread-and-butter punches in MMA. It is a boxing-based straight punch that is always executed with the rear hand to the head, specifically the jaw, and to the body, specifically the solar plexus. The cross along with a lead hook punch, rear hook punch and a rear overhand punch represent the four primary knockout punches in MMA.

Application
Cross to the Head and Body

1. From a southpaw stance, Fighter A stands off against Fighter B.

2. To execute the cross, Fighter A swings his left fist straight out in a pistonlike fashion, using a whipping hip rotation to put his body weight into the blow.

Insights

- When delivering a cross to the body, a fighter still needs to punch straight. This means that he shouldn't punch down but lower his body, by bending his knees, to deliver a straight cross.

- Proper punching form dictates that a fighter must keep his chin tucked down, hands up, elbows in and knees slightly bent, and he also must maintain good balance at all times when executing this or any other strike. Tucking the chin protects the jaw, keeping the elbows in protects the ribs, and bending the knees facilitates good balance and a stable base.

- It's equally important for a fighter to exhale while throwing the punch, strike through the target (and not at it), and retract the punch as rapidly as he shoots it out. Not breathing during a punch is a common problem, which takes away from the strike's power. Striking through is a mental ploy that allows a fighter to psychologically strengthen his punch. The fast retraction augments the faster-than-I-shot-it-out mentality.

3. Because the fist is thrown in a pistonlike fashion, Fighter A can quickly retract and regain his defensive stance.

4. He uses the same techniques to launch a similarly quick and explosive cross at Fighter B's solar plexus.

Additional Information
- ☞ hook (punch)
- ☞ jab
- ☞ overhand (punch)
- ☞ uppercut

CROSS-FACE

Description

The cross-face is a wedge that thwarts an opponent's double- or single-leg takedown. As a defensive wrestling countermove, this technique uses a fighter's forearm as a barrier between the fighter's body and his opponent's head. The wedge allows the competitor to rotate the opponent's head in a direction that is the opposite of his forward driving motion. By cranking his head and putting pressure on his neck, the cross-face prevents an adversary from securing his takedown.

Applications
Cross-Face vs. a Double-Leg Takedown

When Fighter B bridges the gap for a double-leg takedown, Fighter A applies a cross-face with a sprawl to thwart it.

Insights

- The cross-face is a versatile countermove that can effectively thwart takedown attempts from various positions. It can be employed not only in a pushing-type of manner but also more ballistically like a strike. Both ways elicit displacing the opponent's head in a direction opposite to the one he's applying force in.

- A fighter drives the cross-face in a clockwise or counterclockwise rotational manner, depending on which arm is applying the maneuver.

- By rotating the head, the cross-face misaligns the spine.

- When thwarting a double-leg takedown, the cross-face is an integral part of the sprawl. When thwarting a single-leg takedown, a fighter doesn't necessarily have to sprawl but rather wedge his arm and rotate the opponent's head.

Cross-Face vs. a Single-Leg Takedown

1. Fighter B attempts to do a single-leg takedown, and to prevent him, Fighter A uses his right arm to apply a cross-face.

2. With his arm wedged between his body and the opponent's head, Fighter A halts Fighter B's forward motion and takedown attempt.

Additional Information
- ☞ double-leg takedown
- ☞ single-leg takedown
- ☞ sprawl
- ☞ whizzer

CROSSOVER HIP SWEEP

Description

This sweep is a Brazilian *jiu-jitsu* maneuver used to reverse a fighter's position from a guard to the more advantageous mount position. To accomplish the reversal, a competitor sits up and sweeps his mounted opponent clockwise or counterclockwise (depending on which arm the fighter traps and the direction he takes his opponent). By driving and thrusting his hips, the competitor also facilitates his rotation from bottom guard to top mount. The crossover hip sweep is also known as the "*kimura* sweep."

Application
Crossover Hip Sweep From the Closed Guard (Front and Back View)

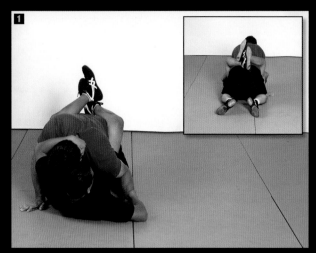

1. Fighter A has Fighter B in the closed guard.

2. Then Fighter A uncrosses his legs and splays them out, posting his left foot on the ground while laying his right leg on its side and next to Fighter B's left leg.

3. Simultaneously, Fighter A sits up, posting on his right hand. He reaches over Fighter B's left shoulder, as if he plans to execute a kimura arm lock.

4. From there, Fighter A immediately thrusts his left hip to the right.

Insights

- The crossover hip sweep is also known as the kimura sweep because a fighter can attempt to do a kimura lock before or after attempting the sweep. That doesn't mean that the fighter needs to attempt the lock in order to do the sweep.

- This is a fundamental guard sweep that, if diligently practiced and timed just right, is a viable one to employ.

- A fighter can also transition to an *omo plata* if his crossover hip sweep is nullified.

5. Concurrently, he pulls and rotates Fighter B in a clockwise direction to reverse him.

6. When the sweep is completed, Fighter A is now on the mount and Fighter B is on the bottom.

7. With a more advantageous position, Fighter A is ready to ground-and-pound.

Additional Information
☞ half-butterfly elevator sweep
☞ kimura
☞ omo plata

CRUCIFIX

Description

The crucifix describes a variety of submission holds in which an opponent's arms are trapped in a crucifixlike position. This disconcerting hold splays the defending fighter's arms outward while cranking his neck back to where tremendous pressure can be exerted on it, causing the opponent to submit or risk a broken neck. The attacking fighter can execute a crucifix hold with his legs, arms or in combination and from many different positions.

Applications
Crucifix From Side Control

1-3. From a side-control position, Fighter A uses his right hand to push Fighter B's left arm up to a perpendicular position in relation to his body. He holds this position momentarily, gripping Fighter B's left shoulder for control.

4. Then Fighter A exerts forward pressure to turn Fighter B onto his left side.

5. Once turned, he continues maintaining the neck crank that naturally occurred in the rotation with the pinning of Fighter B's right arm to Fighter A's left side.

6. This gives Fighter A enough time and space to post his left foot over Fighter B's left arm. The securely pinned left arm and tightly trapped right arm signal that Fighter A can now fall into a crucifix.

7-8. Fighter A immediately lies back and crosses his right leg over his left, placing the crook of his right knee on top of the left ankle to secure leg positioning.

9. Simultaneously, he grabs a hold of his opponent's head with both hands, applying pressure to the neck and spine by pulling Fighter B's head toward Fighter A's head. With the crucifix "locked," Fighter B will either tap in submission from the pain or risk a neck/spine injury.

10. This photo shows the end position for this version of the crucifix from another angle.

Insights

- The crucifix has many steps and variations, which create a greater chance of error in application, especially against a resisting opponent. It also may give an opponent more time to counter. So, like all complicated submission moves, it is imperative to apply it in an explosive and rapid manner. It, of course, has a higher chance of success against an opponent who is unfamiliar with the technique.

- The most devastating display of a crucifix position in an MMA fight occurred when Gary Goodridge trapped Paul Herrera and rendered him unconscious with rapid, repeated downward elbow strikes to the head in the UFC 8 fight.

Crucifix From a Sprawl

1. After countering a double-leg takedown with a sprawl and an underhook with his right arm, Fighter A prepares to execute a crucifix.

2. Immediately thereafter, he scoots his knees up close while maintaining the underhook on Fighter B's arm. From here, Fighter A reaches over Fighter B's back to grasp his hands together, securing a good two-handed grip.

3. Then Fighter A propels himself over Fighter B's back, causing him to roll over onto his back.

4. While doing this, Fighter A hooks Fighter B's right arm with his own right leg (grapevining it in essence).

5. When the competitors become supine, Fighter A immediately reaches up to over-hook Fighter B's arm, trapping it snugly under the armpit. He then wraps his left arm around the back of Fighter B's neck.

6. Fighter A finishes the hold by securing a leg wrap that is similar to a figure-4. In the process of doing the aforementioned, he grabs a hold of his head by clasping his hands together.

7. To apply pressure to his neck, Fighter A pulls Fighter B's head toward his own head while maintaining the crucifix position. This cranks the neck, which will cause Fighter B to either submit or risk injury to his neck.

Additional Information
- ☞ grapevines
- ☞ side control
- ☞ sprawl

D'ARCE CHOKE

Description

The D'Arce choke is a reverse arm-triangle choke and submission hold that is executed from the north/south position against an opponent who is on his hands and knees. He wraps one of his arms underneath the opponent's armpit and neck, where it emerges on the opponent's neck side. Trapping the arm secures the victim and constricts blood flow on one side of his neck, while the aggressor uses his arm to constrict the blood flow to the other side of the victim's neck. The D'Arce choke is also known as the Brabo choke.

Application
D'Arce From a Sprawl

1. To thwart Fighter B's double-leg takedown, Fighter A sprawls with a left overhook/right underhook counter.

2. Driving them into a north/south hands-and-knees position, Fighter A transitions his right underhook into a right overhook over Fighter B's left arm (not shown). This puts Fighter A in a position to thread his arm through for a choke.

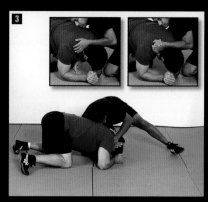

3. From his overhook position, Fighter A slides his right arm underneath Fighter B's armpit and across the underside of Fighter B's neck. Once his hand is out, Fighter A clasps it with a palm-to-palm grip.

4. In this position, Fighter A places his left forearm across the back of Fighter B's neck, using his left forearm like a lever to roll his opponent to his side.

5-6. Pushing down on the back of his neck and rotating his head and upper body in a counterclockwise direction, Fighter A rolls Fighter B onto his right side.

Insights

- Like its cousin the anaconda choke, the D'Arce has more than a few preparatory steps before the choke is locked in. As a result, there is more room for error and for an opponent to counter. As such, this choke needs to be applied with speed and precision to work against a resisting opponent.

- The difference between the anaconda choke and D'Arce is the position of the choking arm. In the anaconda choke, a fighter threads his arm around the opponent's neck by going from the neck side to under the armpit. In the D'Arce choke, the fighter gets his chokehold by threading his arm from under the opponent's armpit to his neck.

- Technically, this choke is actually a stranglehold because it constricts the carotid arteries rather than the windpipe. "Choke" or "blood choke" is just the more commonly applied term in MMA.

- This choke gets its name from a Brazilian *jiu-jitsu* black belt by the name of Joe D'Arce who used this choke successfully in numerous submission-grappling matches.

7. Fighter A releases his palm-to-palm grip once Fighter B is on his side. He then pushes Fighter B's head inward while sliding his own arm farther underneath Fighter B's neck, forcing it in the other direction.

8. Once his hand is jutting out palm-up, Fighter A does a figure-4 hold. He places his palm on his left biceps.

9. He completes the hold by placing his left hand on Fighter B's back. As soon as the figure-4 is "locked" in place, Fighter A finishes his D'Arce choke by squeezing his arms together while sprawling his legs out. This applies downward pressure with his chest and hips, forcing Fighter B to submit or be rendered unconscious.

Additional Information
- ☞ anaconda choke
- ☞ arm triangle
- ☞ overhooks
- ☞ underhooks

DIRTY BOXING CLINCH

Description

The dirty boxing clinch uses a single collar tie-up to maneuver an opponent into vulnerable positions to strike him with hooks, uppercuts and elbows. The tie-up maneuver refers to when a fighter clinches his adversary by the neck with a single hand. Although the clinch's primary purpose is to provide a platform from which to execute strikes, it's also possible to transition into a takedown maneuver.

Application
The Dirty Boxing Clinch in Action

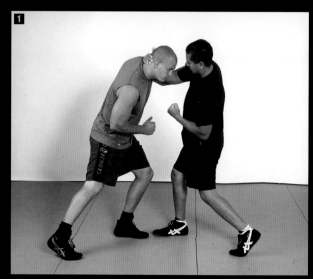

1. Fighter A gets Fighter B in a right-handed collar tie-up.

2. He strikes with a rear uppercut.

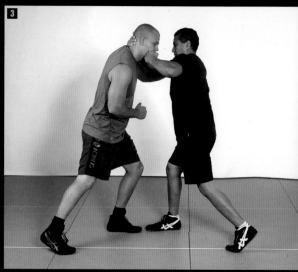

3. Then Fighter A punches with a rear hook.

4. He follows it with a rear inward elbow strike.

Insights

- The illustrations are very static, but in reality, the dirty boxing clinch is extremely dynamic. A fighter executes strikes and keeps the opponent off-balance by pulling at his neck to move him around the mat. This enables the fighter to throw strikes with less resistance from his adversary.

- The dirty boxing clinch is a component of dirty boxing. Dirty boxing gets its name because, in boxing, competitors are not allowed to clinch and hit. If they do, they are separated by the referee.

5-7. To continue his onslaught, Fighter A transitions from a right-hand tie-up to a left-hand tie-up position. Photos 6 and 7 show a different angle.

Additional Information
- ☞ elbow strikes
- ☞ hook (punch)
- ☞ uppercut (punch)

DOUBLE-LEG TAKEDOWN

Description

This is the primary wrestling-based takedown used in MMA, but the most often used method is a modified version of it. In the original, a fighter takes a deep penetrating step to snatch both of the opponent's legs. He then drops his lead knee to the ground as a follow-through to the takedown. In the modified version, the fighter penetrates—closing the gap without dropping his knee—and snatches the opponent's legs to follow through with a pickup and slam to the ground.

Applications
Modified Double-Leg Takedown

1. From unmatched leads, Fighter A throws a right jab to set up his takedown and give it impetus through forward drive and distraction.

2. Immediately after executing the jab, he takes a deep penetration step, bridging the gap. Fighter A grasps the back of Fighter B's upper thighs with both hands.

3. Immediately upon doing so, Fighter A brings his left foot almost next to his right foot. This essentially squares his feet up and establishes close, tight hip contact with Fighter B. It also solidifies Fighter A's base.

4. From here, Fighter A immediately lifts up Fighter B. He does this with his head outside on the left, pressed against the right side of Fighter B's body.

5. To take his adversary down, Fighter A rotates his head and body clockwise. This drives both competitors to the mat but places Fighter A in a good position to transition into side control.

6-7. Fighter A obtains a secure side-control position and immediately drives a straight knee strike into Fighter B's rib cage.

Insights

- This is considered the most essential takedown in MMA and for good reason; it's very effective.

- This takedown, along with the body-lock and single-leg takedown, are the three fundamental takedowns to master for MMA. Along with the body-lock takedown, the double-leg takedown (in all its variants) is the most prevalent and effective one used in MMA.

- By dropping the knee in the original double-leg takedown, a fighter establishes a good base underneath his opponent's center of gravity.

- It's also possible to do a pickup and slam in the original double-leg takedown. It's also possible to do an inside trip as well when an opponent maneuvers his legs in such a way to allow an inside hooking of his foot.

Original Double-Leg Takedown

1. Once again, Fighter A throws a right jab to the opponent's head, setting up his takedown and giving it impetus through forward drive and distraction.

2. Immediately after executing the jab, Fighter A takes a deep penetration step, breaching the distance between him and his adversary.

3. Fighter A closes the gap to tightly secure a double-leg grasp with his hips close in to Fighter B. In doing this, Fighter A penetrates even deeper by dropping his lead knee between Fighter B's legs.

4. With his head outside on the left and pressed against the right side of Fighter B's body, Fighter A steps through and to the outside with his left leg.

7-9. With Fighter B on his back, Fighter A immediately transitions into side control.

5. To finish the takedown, Fighter A uses an outside trip, hooking his own left foot behind Fighter B's right foot from the outside.

6. He takes his adversary down by driving his right shoulder straight through Fighter B's body.

Additional Information
☞ body-lock takedown
☞ single-leg takedown

ELBOW ESCAPE

Description

A fighter performs this fundamental Brazilian *jiu-jitsu* escape by using his elbows as a wedge to escape a mounted opponent. The technique creates enough space for the fighter to shrimp his hips and reverse positions. (A shrimp maneuver is BJJ speak for turning to the side.)

Applications

Elbow Escape to Closed Guard (Side and Front View)

1. With the mounted opponent raining punches, Fighter A keeps his hands up to block the punches.

2. While doing this, Fighter A uses his elbows to scoot up and simultaneously push Fighter B down over his hips.

3. As soon as the opponent is over the hips, Fighter A bucks Fighter B up to off-balance him and displace his base.

4. Once displaced, Fighter A immediately wedges his right elbow to the inside of Fighter B's left knee and places his right hand on Fighter B's left hip.

5. Now Fighter A shrimps his hips and body to the right, creating space to slide his right leg free.

6. Once out, he hooks his right foot over Fighter B's left calf.

7. From there, Fighter A repeats the same escape for the opposite leg. He wedges his left elbow into Fighter B's right inner knee and places his right hand on his right hip. Shrimping his body to create space, Fighter A frees his left leg.

8. Once the left leg is free, Fighter A immediately bring both legs up and over the opponent's back area, crossing them together in a closed-guard position.

9. Simultaneously, he wraps his arms around Fighter B's head, pulling his adversary in tightly to prevent strikes or a guard pass.

Insights

- This is an excellent maneuver to displace a solidly mounted opponent and put him in the more easily defendable guard position. This maneuver should be used alongside the bridging escape, so between the two, a fighter can more easily escape the mount.

- If facing a mounted opponent who is also bigger, the elbow escape is generally more effective than the bridging escape because the fighter doesn't have to lift or buck the heavier adversary off him.

- Even though the name implies that elbows are instrumental to the technique, a fighter can also use his hands to assist in the escape.

- It's always a good idea to have at least two or three techniques to escape the mount in order to alternate maneuvers when one doesn't work. In fact, a fighter can attempt one maneuver as a set up for another one.

Elbow Escape Against a Bigger Opponent

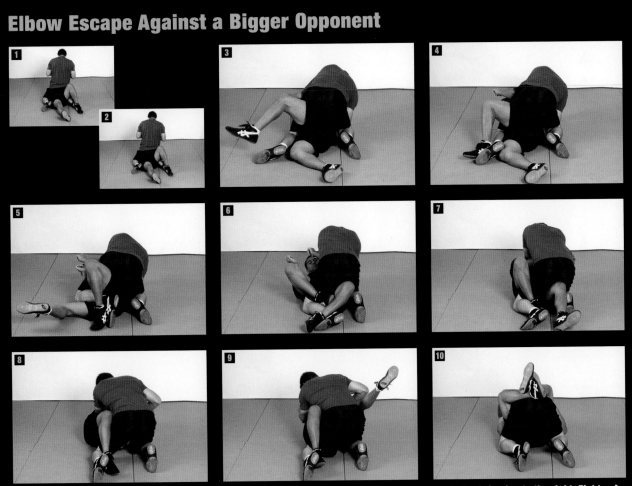

1-10. This shows the same sequence as the previous one but with a key variation. Instead of strictly shrimping to the right, Fighter A crosses his left leg over his right to hook Fighter B's left foot on the outside. This helps Fighter A more easily lift Fighter B's left leg up and slide his own right leg out from underneath it with less resistance. From there, everything else is the same. The steps from the previous examples apply for the rest of the sequence.

Additional Information
☞ bridging escape

ELBOW STRIKES

Description

Elbow strikes are for close-range attacks. The strikes are characterized by inward-horizontal and downward-diagonal trajectories and can be thrown from the stand-up, clinch or ground positions. They mainly target the head but also the body when used on the ground. They can be used in conjunction with other strikes—hooks, crosses or jabs—from any position.

Applications
Left-Horizontal Elbow Strike

1. Fighter A and Fighter B face off in a clinch position.

2. Targeting the jaw, Fighter A throws a left inward-horizontal elbow strike at his opponent's jaw.

Insights

- Elbow strikes are most often executed off the rear side in stand-up and clinch positions. On the ground, fighters can throw elbow strikes from either arm and in various trajectories—inward, outward, upward and downward.

- Like with other punches, it's important for a fighter to punch through his target rather than at it. However, it's not as necessary to quickly retract the elbow strike because its purpose is to knock a rival out with one blow, if possible. In reality, the blow tends to cut more than anything.

- The use of elbows in MMA is somewhat controversial because they don't do much damage but often cause cuts, which can lead to a fight being stopped because of blood loss. This is often considered unfair. For example, let's say that Fighter A is clearly dominating and winning the fight, but suddenly, Fighter B lands an elbow, cutting Fighter A's forehead without hurting him. Despite not being hurt, the attending doctor will usually stop the fight, especially if too much bloodletting is perceived. So even though Fighter A was clearly and decisively winning, the fight would be awarded to Fighter B. This is one reason some promotions don't allow elbow strikes.

- Elbow strikes are more effective on the ground than in stand-up and clinch positions. Because they can seriously hurt and even knock out opponents on the ground, elbow strikes in real-life ground fighting are worthwhile techniques to learn.

- In the UFC, elbow strikes to the head and body are allowed.

Downward-Diagonal Elbow Strike

1. Fighter A and Fighter B face off in a clinch position.

2. Fighter A raises his elbow up to strike downward in a diagonal direction. The oblique angle makes it more difficult for Fighter B to defend against it.

3. Fighter A executes a rear left downward-diagonal elbow strike to his opponent's jaw.

Additional Information
- ☞ dirty boxing clinch
- ☞ ground-and-pound
- ☞ muay Thai clinch

FIGURE-4 HOLDS

Description

Figure-4 is a generic term used to describe holds that look like the numeral four and can be executed by the arms or legs. There are many variations of the figure-4 found in MMA because they can be used to hold an opponent's leg, arm, wrist, etc. The hold usually involves applying pressure on the trapped limb to force the opponent to submit to keep the targeted area from being dislocated. Figure-4 holds are not submission holds per se but rather an important component of them.

Applications
Figure-4 in the Americana

An important step in executing the Americana, Fighter A locks Fighter B's upper arm in a figure-4 wrist lock.

Insights

- Figure-4 holds are sometimes identified as "locks" even though that is technically incorrect. They are holds that are part of locking techniques.

- The term "figure-4" is also interchangeable with "key lock," *"kimura"* and "Americana" in MMA.

Figure-4 in the Kimura

From this angle, it's obvious that Fighter A cannot submit Fighter B without applying a figure-4 hold to his opponent's shoulder.

Figure-4 in an Ankle Lock

Fighter A submits his opponent, with a figure-4 hold ankle lock.

Additional Information
- ☞ Americana
- ☞ ankle locks
- ☞ kimura

FOOT STOMP

Description

The foot stomp is a close-range technique that is often used in the clinch. A fighter stomps downward, using his heel to strike the top of the opponent's instep with whichever foot is best at that moment. The move isn't meant to hurt an opponent. Instead, it distracts him and keeps him on the defensive so the fighter can transition into dirty boxing or go for a takedown. The technique is also known as the "heel stomp."

Application
General Foot-Stomp Scenario

1. The two competitors are in a clinch.

2. To distract his opponent, Fighter A raises his left knee.

Insight

- The higher a fighter raises his knee to start the stomp, the more power he'll generate on impact.

3. He drives his left heel into Fighter B's instep.

Additional Information
☞ dirty boxing clinch

FRONT KICK

Description

The front kick is a straightforward strike executed by the rear or lead leg, depending on preference or situation. Generally, it targets the opponent's midsection, specifically the solar plexus or stomach because they're the most vulnerable kicking targets. It is the second most prevalent kick used in MMA right after the vaunted round kick.

Applications
Rear-Left Front Kick

1. From unmatched leads, Fighter A and Fighter B face off.

2. Fighter A chambers his left knee. He can chamber even if he hasn't taken a momentum-generating step with his right foot.

3. He then thrusts his left foot straight forward and through the opponent's midsection.

Insights

- The front kick can also target the opponent's head but is not done that extensively in MMA.

- In *muay Thai,* a front kick to the face is a sign of disrespect to an opponent because, culturally, it touches the "lowest" body part to the most sacred.

- A front kick with the rear leg is more offensive because it has a longer distance to travel to the target, gaining more momentum and power in the process. A front kick with the lead leg is considered more defensive because it is in a better position to intercept an opponent's attack.

- Even though there are different ways to throw a kick, in MMA a front kick is more like a stomp kick with hip power behind it. This is because any kick in MMA needs substance or else an opponent will be able to walk through it.

Lead-Right Front Kick

The mechanics are exactly the same as throwing it with the rear leg.

Additional Information
- ☞ round kick
- ☞ stomp kick
- ☞ up-kick

GOGO PLATA

Description

The *gogo plata* is the leg choke applied from the rubber guard in which a fighter maneuvers the shin of his high guard leg across the opponent's throat. Simultaneously, he uses both hands to lock the position and pull his adversary in, securing a choke by applying pressure to the adversary's throat with the applied shin. If the opponent does not submit, he will be rendered unconscious.

Application
General Gogo Plata Scenario

1. From a closed-guard position, Fighter A defends against Fighter B's straight punches by parrying them.

2. Using his legs, Fighter A pulls Fighter B in tight. He keeps him close by wrapping his right arm around Fighter B's neck and overhooking his left arm with Fighter B's right arm.

3. Opening his guard, Fighter A works his left leg up into a rubber-guard position.

4. He then quickly transitions into a gogo plata by pulling his own left shin up and over Fighter B's head with his hands.

Insights

- This is one of the newer submissions in MMA pioneered by rubber-guard guru Eddie Bravo.

- Because it's a cousin of the rubber guard, fighters who execute the technique must have pretty flexible hips and legs to maneuver into the position.

- Because the gogo plata requires so much flexibility, it's rarely used successfully during bouts. The most famous example thus far of this submission hold's potency is when Nick Diaz submitted Takanori Gomi with it in PRIDE 33: Second Coming in Las Vegas in February 2007. Shinya Aoki, the premier triangle submission master, has also applied this choke in MMA competition.

- Unlike the D'Arce and anaconda chokes, the gogo plata is technically a chokehold because it cuts off an opponent's air supply rather than blood flow.

5. Immediately after doing this, Fighter A maneuvers his left shin across Fighter B's throat.

6. He secures the choke by grabbing Fighter B's head with both hands and pulling it in while simultaneously pushing his shin against Fighter B's throat. Fighter B can either submit or be rendered unconscious.

Additional Information
- ☞ anaconda choke
- ☞ D'Arce choke
- ☞ parrying
- ☞ rubber guard

GRAPEVINE

Description

The grapevine is a controlling maneuver in which a fighter hooks his heels (singly or doubly) into his opponent's inner thighs. This technique secures and then maintains a back-mount or back-control position, and it gives the fighter a stable base to apply a rear-naked choke from. However, it's possible to grapevine in the mount to prevent bucking or from the bottom-guard position to prevent the opponent from transitioning. A fighter also will do a grapevine in conjunction with underhooks to secure a back-control position.

Applications
Double Grapevine to Stretch an Opponent Out in a Prone Position

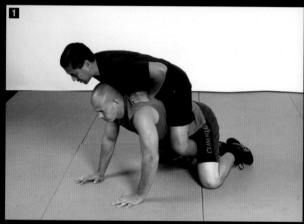

1. Fighter A straddles Fighter B in a back-control position with both his feet grapevining his opponent's inner thighs.

2. He thrusts his hips forward while simultaneously extending his legs forcefully back.

3. This breaks down Fighter B's hands-and-knees position by stretching him out.

4. Once Fighter B is prone, Fighter A can work a ground-and-pound attack or transition into a rear-naked choke.

Insights

- The use of grapevines is crucial in establishing and maintaining a back-control position over an opponent. In conjunction with the use of underhooks and overhooks, grapevines allow a fighter to stick to an opponent in back control like a leach no matter how the opponent moves and rolls.

- If necessary, a fighter in a back mount can keep his opponent prone by continually exerting downward pressure with his own hips and by thrusting them.

- The most common submission executed with grapevines and a back-control position is the rear-naked choke because the fighter is in a natural position to execute that hold.

- "Putting the hooks in" is slang for grapevines.

- A fighter can apply them, not only from a prone or supinated back-control position, but also from a mount position to thwart off a bottom opponent's attempt to bridge.

Double Grapevine With Underhooks

1. To main his back-control position, Fighter A does a double grapevine with underhooks on Fighter B from a seated position.

2. This shows his position from a different angle.

Additional Information
- ☞ bridging escape
- ☞ mount
- ☞ overhooks
- ☞ rear-naked choke
- ☞ underhooks

GROUND AND POUND

Description

Ground and pound is a core ground-fighting tactic: A fighter applies strikes to his opponent while on the ground. The fighter controls his rival from a top position—side control, mount, back mount, from inside the guard or top guard—and blasts him with punches, hammerfists, elbows and knees. In essence, the purpose of this tactic is to just knock the opponent out or beat him into submission.

Applications
Ground and Pound From the Mount

1-6. Fighter A grounds-and-pounds Fighter B from a mount position. He starts off with a straight punch and follows it up with an inward-horizontal elbow strike and then a downward elbow strike.

Ground and Pound From Inside the Closed Guard

1-5. In a standing position, Fighter A grounds-and-pounds his opponent from inside his closed guard. He maintains his dominant position by pinning Fighter B's arm with his right hand. Then Fighter A launches a left straight punch to Fighter B's face followed by a left downward elbow to his midsection.

Insights

- This tactic was pioneered and popularized by Mark Coleman and Tito Ortiz.

- Common counters to defending against the ground and pound are covering or wrapping the antagonist's arms and head to pull him in close and stop the blows. If the antagonist is in side control and applying knee strikes, the defending fighter will try to put him in the guard.

- It's still considered a ground and pound if the attacker is on his knees and as long as his opponent is prone or supine.

Ground and Pound From Side Control

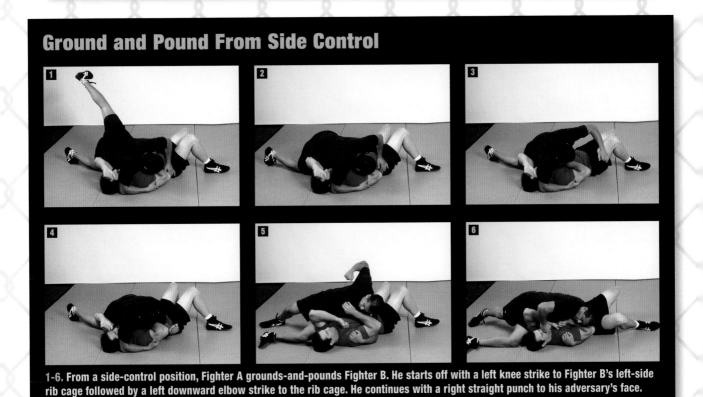

1-6. From a side-control position, Fighter A grounds-and-pounds Fighter B. He starts off with a left knee strike to Fighter B's left-side rib cage followed by a left downward elbow strike to the rib cage. He continues with a right straight punch to his adversary's face.

Additional Information
- ☞ arm wrap
- ☞ cross (punch)
- ☞ elbow strikes
- ☞ hook (punch)
- ☞ jab (punch)
- ☞ knee strikes
- ☞ mount
- ☞ overhand (punch)
- ☞ side control
- ☞ top guard
- ☞ uppercut (punch)

GUILLOTINE CHOKE

Description

The guillotine choke is one of the bread-and-butter submissions in MMA. It is a front head lock applied from a stand-up position, the closed guard, the half-guard or the mount. It can be performed two ways: by encircling the neck, or by encircling the neck and overhooking an arm. This is a versatile chokehold that can be applied in a myriad of ways from a variety of positions as long as both competitors are face-to-face.

Applications
Guillotine Choke No. 1

1. Fighter A thwarts Fighter B's double-leg takedown attempt with a sprawl and cross-face.

2. He then transitions into a guillotine choke by encircling his left arm around Fighter B's neck. Fighter A keeps his encircled forearm tight across his opponent's throat.

3. To secure the chokehold, Fighter A grips his left wrist with his right hand. While doing this, he also transitions into a knees-on-the-deck position.

4. During the transition, Fighter A also lifts and squeezes his arms tightly around Fighter B's neck, using a hip thrust to tighten the choke.

5. Maintaining the chokehold, Fighter A rotates his opponent to the ground so that Fighter B hits the mat prone.

6-7. When he is prone, Fighter A immediately takes the mount position and applies even more pressure to his neck by lifting Fighter B's head up. In conjunction to tightly squeezing his opponent's arms, Fighter A causes Fighter B to submit by tapout or be rendered unconscious.

Additional Information
☞ anaconda choke
☞ D'Arce choke
☞ rear-naked choke

Insights

- This is one of the two primary chokeholds (the other one being the rear-naked choke) in MMA.

- It's not unusual to see a fighter use this chokehold while thwarting a takedown because it puts him in a natural, face-to-face position in which to execute it.

- It's possible to submit opponents with the guillotine while standing up.

- Interestingly enough, it is a technique converted kickboxers, such as Mirko "Cro Cop" Filipovic and Alistair Overeem, gravitate to and use effectively in MMA fights.

- Unlike the anaconda choke or D'Arce choke, the guillotine is actually a "choke" or "air choke" because it constricts a person's airway rather than blood flow.

Guillotine Choke No. 2 With an Overhooked Arm (Back and Side View)

1. From a closed-guard position, Fighter A blocks Fighter B's punches before pulling him into a tight clinch. He releases the closed guard to transition into a kimura.

2-3. In this particular instance, Fighter B counters the kimura attempt.

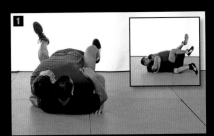

4. Fighter A immediately decides to transition into a guillotine. He sits up, scooting himself back into a seated upright position.

5. He encircles his left arm around Fighter B's neck.

6. He also overhooks his right arm with Fighter B's left arm.

7. Then Fighter A positions the wrist of the encircled arm on Fighter B's throat, gripping it with his own right hand at the same time.

8. Applying the neck-and-arm version of the guillotine, Fighter A lies back, pulling up on his arms while simultaneously extending his legs out in the opposite direction.

9. If applied correctly, Fighter B will tap in submission or be rendered unconscious.

HALF-BUTTERFLY ELEVATOR SWEEP

Description

This reversal is a Brazilian *jiu-jitsu* technique. From the full-butterfly guard, the fighter displaces his mounted opponent by sweeping him with a half-butterfly maneuver. The half-butterfly maneuver is when a fighter removes one foot from the full-butterfly guard and places it outside the opponent's leg. He pushes with the inside foot and pulls with the outside foot, creating a scissor motion that rotates the opponent from the mount to bottom position. This reversal is also known as the "butterfly elevator sweep" even though it is always executed in a half-butterfly position.

Application
General Scenario for Half-Butterfly Elevator Sweep

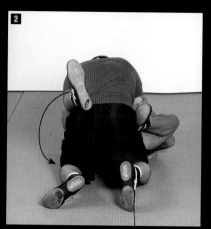

1. Fighter A holds a mounted Fighter B in the closed guard.

2-3. He transitions into a butterfly guard by placing the insteps of his feet on Fighter B's inner thighs, one foot at a time.

4-5. He places each foot one at a time; the right foot is followed by the left foot.

6. Once a butterfly guard has been obtained, Fighter A knocks Fighter B off-balance by pulling Fighter B forward and lifting Fighter B up with his own legs.

Insights

- The "elevator" part of the move refers to when a fighter lifts an opponent up into the air with his legs.

- With the all-around skills reaching a level of parity in MMA, guard sweeps haven't been as viable as they once were in the past. However, this is one sweep that can still be effectively used if a fighter is able to displace his opponent's base, changing his center of gravity, and keeping him in close. It then becomes a matter of redirecting his weight through a semi-scissoring action with the fighter's legs.

7. With Fighter B's base displaced, Fighter A quickly takes his left foot out of the butterfly position and into a half-butterfly position. He hooks the free foot against Fighter B's right leg (by his right knee).

8. Fighter A immediately lifts Fighter B's left leg up with his right foot and sweeps Fighter B's right leg with his left foot in a scissor motion, rotating them both counterclockwise.

9-10. Now the competitors positions are reversed, placing Fighter A in the mount and ready to ground-and-pound Fighter B.

Additional Information
☞ butterfly guard
☞ scissor sweep

HALF-GUARD

Description

The half-guard is a variation of the fundamental guard position in which the fighter only has one leg around the opponent instead of both. Usually, a competitor uses the half-guard to stop an opponent who is trying to pass the guard or obtain a better position like side control or the mount. From the half-guard, he then usually tries to maneuver back into a full-guard position.

Application
Two Perspectives of the Half-Guard

1. Rear view of Fighter A adopting a half-guard position on his opponent's left leg.

Insights

- There are two basic ways to pass an opponent's half-guard. The first is to post the trapped leg and use the complementary hand to pull it out of the guard. The second is to use the free leg as a wedge to push and pull the trapped leg out.

- The half-guard is also a viable position to work escape and reversals as well as certain submission holds, like the guillotine choke, arm triangle and *kimura*.

2. Front view of Fighter A adopting a half-guard position on his opponent's left leg.

Additional Information
☞ closed guard
☞ open guard

HAMMERFISTS

Description

These hammer-shaped punches are primal, powerful strikes meant to immobilize or knock out a grounded opponent. It is one of the core strikes used in grounding and pounding. While it can be used in a variety of directions, it is most prevalently used in a downward trajectory.

Applications
General Hammerfist Scenario

1. Fighter A is in the mount, grounding-and-pounding Fighter B, who has his back on the ground.

2. Fighter A launches a hammerfist with his left hand. He raises it high to use distance and gravity to generate a powerful impact.

3. He targets and hits Fighter B's face.

Hammerfist From a Knee-on-Stomach Position

 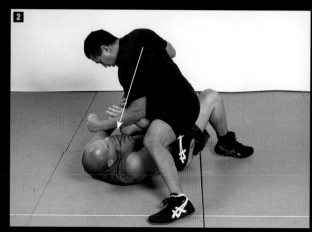

1. From the knee-on-stomach position, Fighter A raises his fist to launch a strike.

2. The hammerfist hits Fighter B in the face.

Insights

- Even though it's possible to use hammerfists while standing, it's not generally done in MMA. Instead, it's a frequently used hand strike on the ground.

- Even though the strike is quite telegraphic, it doesn't matter because the opponent is being barraged.

- To use hammerfists, the opponent has to be on his back. It's also OK to use hammerfists against a prone adversary, but it is more difficult to execute correctly. That's because a fighter can only hit the side of the head. Striking at the back of the head or neck is against MMA rules.

Hammerfist From a Scarf Hold

1. Fighter A transitions from side control to a scarf-hold position.

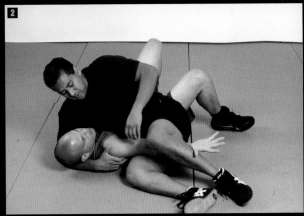

2. He grabs his opponent's arm and traps it by sandwiching it between his legs.

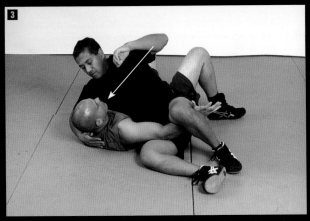

3. With Fighter B's right arm trapped, Fighter A blasts him with a hammerfist to his face.

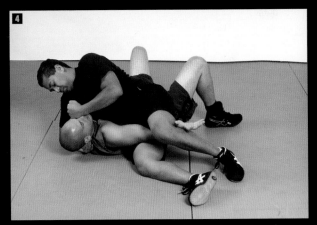

4. He can continue throwing hammerfists or other strikes from this position.

Additional Information
☞ knee on stomach
☞ scarf hold

HEEL HOOKS

Description

The heel hook has a potent and injurious history as a submission hold. A fighter executes it when he secures his supine opponent's heel underneath his armpit while trapping the leg of the secured heel between his legs. From this position, the fighter rotates the heel outward (clockwise or counterclockwise, depending on which foot is secured) to torque the knee for a submission or to break it. It can be applied on the same side or from the opposite side; the opposite side is known as the "reverse" heel hook.

Applications
General Heel-Hook Scenario

1. From inside the opponent's guard position, Fighter A forces Fighter B to open his legs up through a ground-and-pound attack with straight punches to the face.

2. When the distraction works, Fighter A overhooks his arm around Fighter B's right ankle, wrapping it tightly.

3. Immediately after doing this, he falls back into a supine position, squeezing his knees together.

4. To further secure the hold on Fighter B's ankle, Fighter A squeezes the trapped foot tightly underneath his left armpit. He continues to immobilize his opponent's trapped leg by crossing his own left leg over it and squeezing both of his legs together.

5. With his hold secured, Fighter A is ready to maneuver into a heel hook. He positions his left inner forearm underneath and around his opponent's right heel.

6. He then clasps his hands together in a palm-to-palm grip.

7. With the grip secured, Fighter A immediately rotates his arm and body to the right while immobilizing Fighter B's straightened, locked-out position. This puts tremendous torquing pressure on Fighter B's knee, which will cause him to tap out.

Insights

- This submission hold is banned in many MMA organizations because of its injury potential. What makes it so dangerous is that there is no feeling of pain until it is too late and the damage is done. And when the damage is done, the damage is often severe and debilitating, putting a fighter out of commission for a long time.

- While both versions of the heel hook are deadly, the reverse heel hook is considered the more potent of the two because it applies torque in a more awkward angle and is harder to escape from.

- Speaking of which, the basic way to counter heel hooks is for a fighter to spin in the direction of the torquing pressure and to simultaneously use his free leg to push-kick the opponent's butt (literally), augmenting the escape of the trapped foot.

- Masakazu Imanari is the Japanese MMA fighter best known for his use of leg locks, especially heel hooks.

General Reverse Heel-Hook Scenario

1. Instead of placing the ankle under his left armpit for a regular heel hook (face-to-face, the same side), Fighter A maneuvers Fighter B's right ankle under his right armpit (face-to-face, the opposite side).

2. He then turns the right ankle to the left, using his left hand to expose the right heel in an outward position.

3. As he exposes the heel, Fighter A hooks his inner forearm underneath Fighter B's right heel and locks it in with a palm-to-palm grip.

4. Once the heel is hooked in tightly, Fighter A squeezes his legs together and rotates his right arm and body to the left (counter-clockwise), increasing torque pressure on the heel. The opponent must tap out or risk severe knee damage.

Additional Information
☞ ankle lock

HIP ESCAPE/SIDE ESCAPE

Description

The hip escape is a fundamental Brazilian *jiu-jitsu* escape that involves maneuvering an opponent out of side control into the guard or a bottom face-to-face position. A fighter accomplishes this by shrimping, or turning his hips to the side, creating space to escape. The term "hip escape" is interchangeable with "side escape."

Applications
Hip Escape to the Closed Guard

1. Fighter A is in a supine position, and Fighter B is in a left side-control position.

2. To create space, Fighter A shrimps to the left. He simultaneously maneuvers his hips away from Fighter B and slides his left leg underneath Fighter B's body. He also places his hand on Fighter B's hip to help create space.

3. To further facilitate this movement, Fighter A places his left shin across Fighter B's knees. This helps Fighter A push off to straighten his body out as his left leg slides through.

4. From there, Fighter A pulls his left leg out from underneath.

5. As he does so, he brings his right leg up, crossing his ankles, placing Fighter B in a closed guard.

6. During that lower-body maneuvering, Fighter A slides his right arm underneath his opponent's right armpit and wraps it around Fighter B's neck.

7. Now Fighter B is locked in an arm triangle.

Insights

- Both demonstrated maneuvers are fundamental BJJ escapes from a side-control position.
- The key element to executing a successful side escape is creating space through the hip shrimping maneuver. The hips are everything when effecting escapes and reversals from disadvantageous positions.

Side Escape to Side Control

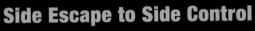

1. Fighter A is supine, and Fighter B is in a side-control position.

2. To escape, Fighter A shrimps to the left, creating space with his hips to maneuver out of his bottom position.

3. Instead of turning in to put his opponent in the guard, Fighter A slides his left leg out and around.

4-6. He then executes a double-leg takedown by wrapping his arms around Fighter B's legs to knock Fighter B to the ground.

7. Now Fighter A can transition into a left side-control position while Fighter B is supine.

Additional Information
- ☞ arm triangle
- ☞ closed guard
- ☞ double-leg takedown
- ☞ side control

HIP THROWS

Description

Hip throws are a category of throws that are executed by head locks, arms around the waist or an underhooked arm. A fighter performs the throws by closing the distance between his opponent and positioning his hips underneath the opponent's body. By pulling the opponent in close, a fighter then rotates his hips and throws the opponent's body over him and to the ground. Hip throws are also an interchangeable term for judo throws. They're recognizable because the attacking fighter can't perform a throw unless his back is to his opponent.

Applications
Hip Throw From a Head Lock

1. From a clinch position, Fighter A obtains a head lock on Fighter B while controlling Fighter B's left arm with his right hand.

2. To do a hip throw, Fighter A steps in and across Fighter B, positioning the backside of his hips next to his opponent's hips. This establishes a stable and square base from which to execute the throw.

3-4. From this position, Fighter A pulls down and rotates his upper body to the right. He simultaneously bends forward at the waist and uses his hips as a fulcrum to throw his opponent over his body, tossing the opponent to the ground.

5. Once grounded, Fighter A pins Fighter B down in a scarf-hold position and begins maneuvering for submission or prepares to ground-and-pound him.

Insights

- While hip throws aren't as prevalent as double-leg and body-lock takedowns, they are nevertheless an effective means of dynamically putting an opponent to the ground. Fighters such as Karo Parisyan and Georges St. Pierre, among others, have effectively used them in competition.

- When employing hip throws, it's crucial to get in tight against the opponent. In essence, a fighter tries to get his hips underneath the opponent's hips in a stable base. This gives the fighter the mechanical leverage to dynamically throw his adversary without much resistance in return.

Hip Throw From Around the Waist

1-2. With his left arm hugging Fighter B's torso and his right arm controlling Fighter B's left arm, Fighter A performs a hip throw

Hip Throw With an Underhook

1-2. By underhooking Fighter B's left arm, Fighter A obtains a stable base from which to perform a hip throw.

Additional Information
- ☞ body-lock takedown
- ☞ double-leg takedown
- ☞ scarf hold
- ☞ underhooks

HOOK (PUNCH)

Description

The hook punch, along with the rear cross and rear overhand, is one of the core, bread-and-butter punches utilized in MMA. It's a boxing-based bent arm, horizontal, outside-in curved punch directed to the head (jaw) and body (ribs, liver, spleen). It is executed with either hand in the lead and rear positions. It is the most potent knockout punch in MMA or boxing because, when hitting the jaw, it torques the brainstem and rattles the brain. The hook punch can be thrown parallel to the ground or at a variation of angles, depending on the opponent's position.

Applications
Rear and Lead Hook Punch

1. From unmatched leads, Fighter A executes a lead right hook to Fighter B's jaw. The power of the punch is generated through a concept known as kinetic linking.

2. From unmatched leads, Fighter A executes a rear left hook to Fighter B's jaw. Power is generated in exactly the same way as the lead hook punch, but instead of rotating counterclockwise, in this instance, Fighter A rotates his body in a clockwise direction.

Shovel Hook

1-2. Fighter A delivers a rear left hook to Fighter B's body. Technically, this punch is known as a shovel hook because it's executed at a 45-degree angled trajectory instead of parallel to the ground. It's technically a body shot, although fighters are known to use it on different targets.

Insights

- It's very important that when a fighter throws this or any other punch, that he throws it at the right range (proper distance) because it can leave him open and vulnerable to a counterattack.

- The fighter must keep his nonstriking hand up in a guard position to protect his jaw and to retract the striking hand faster, then shoot it out to add to the overall impetus of the blow.

- This punch, as with most punches, can be utilized in a variety of different positions, not just in the stand-up phase. A fighter execute punches in a clinch, from the mount, side control, back control, basically any position in which he has a face-to-face or face-to-body position.

- Even more power can be generated with this, or any punch, by taking a momentum-initiating "trigger step" in the direction that the blow travels. This is not shown in any of the photos.

- Kinetic linking generates the hook punch's power. It involve a sequential torque that consists of a ball-of-foot pivot, hip-whip rotation, immediately followed in milliseconds with a recoiled slingshotlike shoulder drive, all done in the same direction. Additionally, the torque is accompanied with a short, sharp exhalation and a follow-through, which means a fighter strikes through and not at the target.

Hooks From the Mount

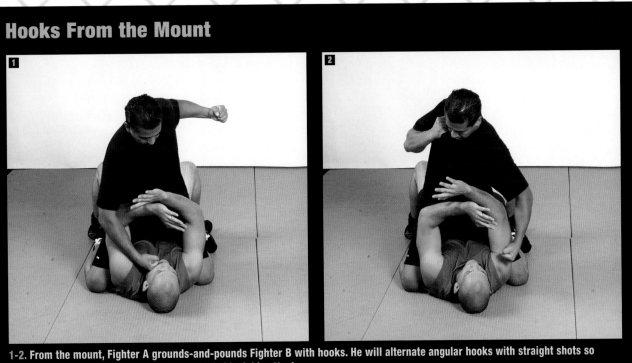

1-2. From the mount, Fighter A grounds-and-pounds Fighter B with hooks. He will alternate angular hooks with straight shots so Fighter B won't be able to read and accurately block his attacks.

Additional Information
- ☞ cross (punch)
- ☞ jab (punch)
- ☞ overhand (punch)
- ☞ uppercut (punch)

JAB (PUNCH)

Description

The jab is a boxing-based lead straight punch in which the lead hand targets the opponent's head and/or body. A fighter delivers and generates power for the punch by pushing off with his rear foot while simultaneously taking a forward step with his lead foot. The jab is used for offense, defense and setting up or in combination with powerful punches and kicks, like the potent cross. Jabs are also used to intercept a strike by making impact with the opponent before his strike impacts the fighter.

Applications
Jab to the Head

1. Fighter A and Fighter B face off in unmatched leads.

2. Fighter A launches a jab by pushing off with his rear foot and taking a trigger step with his lead.

3. His jab strikes Fighter B's chin.

Insights

- The forward step is known as the "trigger step."

- It's equally important for a fighter to always exhale while throwing the punch, strike through the target (and not at it), and retract the punch as rapidly as he shoots it out. Not breathing during a punch is a common problem, which takes away from the strike's power. Striking through is a mental ploy that allows a fighter to psychologically strengthen his punch. The fast retraction augments the faster-than-I-shot-it-out mentality.

- Fighters like Georges St. Pierre and B.J. Penn use the jab to keep an opponent at bay and to set up their offense.

Jab to the Body

Fighter A connects his jab with Fighter B's solar plexus. The method of delivery is the same as when throwing the shot to the head except that Fighter A bends at the knees and not at the waist. He wants to lower his body in order to throw the jab in a straight, parallel-to-the-ground line through the target.

Additional Information
- ☞ cross (punch)
- ☞ hook (punch)
- ☞ overhand (punch)
- ☞ uppercut (punch)

KIMURA

Description

The *kimura* is a submission hold that traps the wrist and cranks the shoulder in a figure-4 hold. It can be applied from the guard, side-control or north/south position. The hold can also be applied by a fighter in an upright position as a counter to a rear-body lock. What distinguishes it from the Americana is its downward rather than upward L-shape.

Applications
Kimura From Closed Guard

1. From a closed-guard position, Fighter A blocks Fighter B's left-handed punch while using his legs to off-balance Fighter B.

2. When he loses his balance, Fighter B falls forward, setting his hand on the ground to regain it. This gives Fighter A the opportunity to grip Fighter B's wrist.

3-4. Fighter A moves into the kimura—he opens his guard and reaches his arm over and around Fighter B's shoulder, overhooking it. Fighter A then grasps his own right wrist with his left hand in a figure-4 hold.

5. When the hold is cinched, Fighter A immediately turns to his left, posting both feet on the ground and forcing his opponent's arm up and to the center of Fighter B's back. He obtains a downward L-shape.

6. As soon as Fighter B hits the mat, Fighter A slides his hips free and turns his body to the left in order to throw his right leg over Fighter B's back. He also continues to drive his opponent's trapped arm into Fighter B's back.

7. Explosively, Fighter A continues twisting the shoulder, which will force Fighter B to tap out or sustain a dislocated shoulder.

Insights

- It's most common to see the kimura executed from side control.

- No matter how he executes the hold, the fighter needs to keep the opponent's arm bent at a 90-degree angle to secure the lock properly. If the fighter doesn't, the opponent can counter the hold by bending his arm toward his own head or stretching his arm out. The 90-degree angle also helps apply the most torque.

Kimura From Side Control

1. From side control, Fighter A softens his opponent with an elbow to the head.

2. During the distraction, Fighter A grabs hold of Fighter B's wrist and pins it to the ground. He also slides his left hand underneath the downward L-shaped arm.

3. Fighter A grabs his right wrist with his own left hand, securing a figure-4 hold.

4. When the hold is secure, Fighter A lifts up Fighter B's shoulder and drives it toward Fighter B's head. Fighter A turns to the left to torque the shoulder more, causing fighter be to tap out.

5. Fighter A can crank the arm more by stepping and posting his left foot over Fighter B's head.

Additional Information
☞ Americana
☞ closed guard
☞ figure-4 holds
☞ north/south position
☞ side control

Kimura From North/South

1. From a north/south position, Fighter A grabs Fighter B's wrist.

2. He pins Fighter B's arm in a downward L-shaped position before transitioning his right hand to securely hold the arm.

3. Once pinned, Fighter A immediately slides his left hand underneath Fighter B's upper arm to secure a figure-4 hold.

4. To secure the hold, Fighter A grabs his own wrist with his left hand.

5. Then Fighter A posts his left leg beside Fighter B's head and pulls up on the opponent's trapped arm.

6. Fighter A pulls up on the arm, raising Fighter B off the ground. He explosively rotates the trapped arm, driving it in the direction of Fighter B's head to force the submission.

KNEEBAR

Description

The kneebar is a leg-lock submission directed at one of the opponent's knees. A fighter traps one knee between his legs and applies pressure to the trapped and straightened knee by thrusting forward with his pelvic area and arching back at the same time. The kneebar can be applied from side-control, open-guard or top-guard positions. In this submission hold, a fighter uses his hands to hold the back of the opponent's shin to his chest to keep the knee straight and get more leverage.

Application
General Scenario for a Kneebar

1. From side control, Fighter B raises his right knee to prevent Fighter A from transitioning into the mount.

2. So instead of pursuing that course of action, Fighter A takes advantage of Fighter B's raised right knee and hooks the crook of that knee with his right hand.

3. Upon doing so, Fighter A immediately props up and places his knee on his opponent's belly.

4. He then wraps up Fighter B's right leg with both his arms (at the crooks of the elbows), pinning it tightly against his own chest to immobilize it.

Insights

- A kneebar is an effective submission hold. However, one of its weaknesses is that if it fails, it puts the fighter in a very disadvantageous position. With any leg lock that fails, a fighter risks the opponent getting free and scrambling into a better position faster than him. This is why fighters often try to address those contingencies during practice so they'll be prepared and have "answers" if or when it happens in competition.

- A fighter counters a kneebar by bending his leg and pulling it to his body while rolling into the lock. He wants to avoid having his knee trapped on his attacker's pelvis because that is where the torque will be applied.

- The kneebar often fails because the attacking fighter doesn't put the knee over his pelvic area and/or secure the leg tightly.

5. Fighter A immediately proceeds to fall back and lie supine with Fighter B's straightened right leg pinned against his own body.

6. On landing, Fighter A crosses his left leg under his right leg and pushes on his opponent's left inner thigh to further immobilize the leg. It also prevents Fighter B from turning into Fighter A to counter the bar.

7. Fighter A rolls to the side to lock the bar.

8. Then he thrusts his hips forward while arching his back slightly to put pressure on Fighter B's knee. Fighter B will need to submit or risk a fractured knee.

Additional Information
- ☞ knee on stomach
- ☞ open guard
- ☞ side control
- ☞ top guard

KNEE ON STOMACH

Description

The knee on stomach is a dominant ground-fighting position in which a fighter attains a good base to ground-and-pound his opponent. The position is usually attained from side control or during a transition from the standing phase to the ground because of a takedown, strike, etc. The fighter controls a supine opponent by placing one of his knees across his rival's stomach. To stabilize the position, he posts his free leg on the ground. The term is interchangeable with "knee on belly."

Applications
Knee on Stomach (Front View)

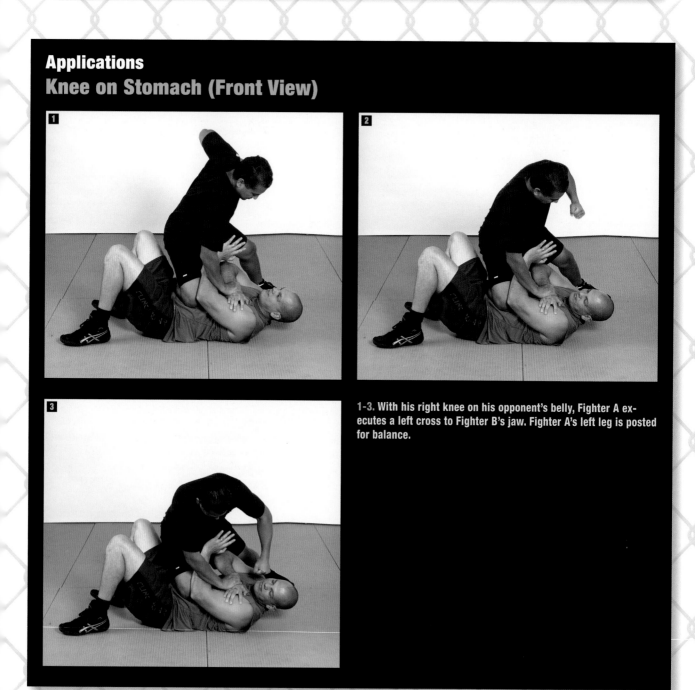

1-3. With his right knee on his opponent's belly, Fighter A executes a left cross to Fighter B's jaw. Fighter A's left leg is posted for balance.

Insights

- It's very important that when utilizing this position, a fighter keeps his hips centered underneath his body. This maintains good posture and makes the opponent feel and carry all the fighter's weight.

- Besides this position being conducive to grounding-and-pounding an opponent with punches, it's also a good one to transition into an armbar should the opponent be foolish enough to extend his near arm defensively.

Knee on Stomach (Side View)

1-2. With his right knee on his opponent's belly, Fighter A punches Fighter B in the face.

Additional Information
☞ armbar
☞ cross (punch)
☞ ground and pound

KNEE STRIKES

Description

These strikes are executed by the fighter's rear knees in a straight, angular, upward, round, side, or jumping-upward trajectory. Knee strikes are versatile and can be employed in the stand-up free-movement phase, clinch phase or ground phase of combat. In the standing phase, they are most often applied from a *muay Thai* neck clinch. On the ground, knee strikes can be used by the top or bottom opponent; the top opponent will usually use them in side control. Power in a knee strike is generated by a rapid thrusting of the hips in the direction of the blow.

Applications
Knee Strikes to the Head

1-2. From a muay Thai neck clinch, Fighter A executes a rear left upward-straight knee strike to the opponent's head.

3-4. He then executes a rear left upward-side knee strike to the right side of the opponent's face. He bends Fighter B slightly to the left to facilitate the strike.

5. Fighter A lands a straight knee strike to Fighter B's head from another position (arms outstretched, hands on top of his head to stabilize it).

Insights

- Knee strikes are the weapons of choice in a clinch situation, and while the body (specifically the ribs and solar plexus) and legs (specifically, the outer and inner thighs) are viable targets, the most sought-after one is the head because it can knockout an opponent. (See Anderson Silva's UFC fights for proof.)
- Knee strikes are only allowed to the head when in stand-up or clinch positions. When on the ground, knee strikes are only allowed to the body.

Knee Strikes to the Body

1. From a muay Thai neck clinch, Fighter A connects with a straight knee strike to the opponent's body (specifically, his solar plexus).

2. Here, Fighter A connects another variation of the standing knee strike to Fighter B's rib cage.

Knee Strikes From a Scarf Hold

1-2. From a scarf-hold position, Fighter A executes an angled right straight knee strike to the supine opponent's head. (Note: This move is prohibited in most organizations.

Knee Strikes From Side Control

1. From a left side-control position, Fighter A prepares to strike.

2. He executes a left straight knee strike to Fighter B's rib cage.

Additional Information
☞ muay Thai clinch

LEG CHECKING

Description

A fighter uses leg checking as a defensive maneuver against kicks. By using his shins or knees, a fighter is able to block and check attacks. Generally, the term "leg checking" is used only when a competitor is standing, but technically, a fighter can leg-check in other positions, too.

Applications
Outward Leg Checks

1-2. Fighter A leg-checks Fighter B's right and left round kicks. The block is "outward" because he is directing his leg check outwardly, away from the centerline of his body.

Insights

- A fighter mostly leg-checks with his lead rather than rear leg. He will also most likely employ the leg check against round kicks.

- When launching a kick, an opponent purposefully targets the thigh area. This means a fighter should never leg-check with his thigh. He should instead use his shins or knees to block kicks.

- Whenever a fighter is defending against leg kicks, he tries not to use his arms or hands because he risks getting nailed in the head when his arms are lowered.

Inward Leg Checks

1-2. Fighter A leg-checks Fighter B's right and left round kicks. The leg checks are "inward" because Fighter A is directing his leg check inwardly, towards the centerline of his body.

Additional Information
☞ round kick

MOUNT

Description

Along with back and side control, the mount is one of the three dominant ground-fighting positions in MMA. In the mount, one competitor is supine while the other straddles him on his knees. Ideally, the mounted fighter wants to be scooted up underneath his opponent's armpits because the opponent won't be able to off-balance him as effectively. The mount is an advantageous position in which to ground-and-pound and/or seek submissions from.

Applications
Mount With a Transition to an Armbar

1-6. Fighter A is mounted on Fighter B, grounding-and-pounding his opponent with straight punches. He takes the opportunity to transition into an armbar and submit Fighter B.

Ideal Mount Position

This is the ideal mount position because Fighter A is riding high on Fighter B's chest with both knees underneath and touching Fighter B's armpits. In this position, any bucking attempt on his part to off-balance Fighter A is an exercise in futility.

Additional Information
☞ armbar
☞ back control
☞ side control

Insights

- Before doing anything offensive from the mount, a fighter needs to establish a good base by sliding and keeping his knees underneath the opponent's armpits. This is the best position to ground-and-pound from the mount.

- If an opponent maneuvers a fighter over his hips, the fighter can also use the grapevine position to prevent himself from being bucked off-balance.

- Though not shown, the mount is an excellent position to throw elbow strikes from.

- An excellent ground-and-pound attack from the mount consists of mixing straight punches and hooks with elbow strikes in order to overwhelm the opponent so that he can't cope with a defense.

- The only advantage that an opponent stuck in the mount has is that he can see what his mounted attacker is doing. In the back mount, a bottom opponent is pretty much helpless.

- When a bottom opponent attempts to trap a mounted fighter's arms with overhooks or underhooks, the mounted fighter can do what's known as "swimming the arms" to keep them from being immobilized.

Mount Counter

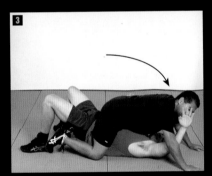

1-3. Instead of under his opponent's armpits, Fighter A is over Fighter B's hips. Fighter B keeps Fighter A there by gluing his elbows into his sides. This is the ideal counter-position for the opponent to maneuver a mounted attacker out of the position. Fighter B can knock Fighter A off-balance by "bucking" his hips upward, causing Fighter A to fall forward and open himself up to attack.

Maintaining the Mount

1-3. To counter Fighter B's attempts to keep him back, Fighter A lifts his opponent's elbows up. He slides his knees back to the underneath-the-armpits position, thus re-establishing a strong mount. This is relatively easy to do, but a fighter who is grounding-and-pounding may not notice that his opponent is pushing him off the mount.

MUAY THAI CLINCH

Description

This clinch from *muay Thai* is a two-handed clasp around the back of the head. A fighter uses it to pull the opponent's chin down to his chest, weakening his posture and making the opponent easier to manipulate. The clinch interlaces the fighter's two hands around the opponent's head and squeezes his two forearms along the opponent's neck. The muay Thai clinch is the preferred position to throw knee strikes from, although it's possible to transition into a takedown, as well. It also thwarts any attempts by the clinched opponent to execute takedowns.

Applications
Muay Thai Clinch With Knee Strikes

1. With his two hands clamped around the opponent's neck, Fighter A has Fighter B in a muay Thai clinch. Note how Fighter B's head is positioned on Fighter A's shoulder. This is the optimal placement for a knee strike.

2. Fighter A pulls down on Fighter B's head, bringing Fighter B's chin downward and his own knee upward and through the target. Fighter A shoots his knee up by rapidly thrusting his hips in the direction of the blow for optimal power.

3. Fighter A can also execute a left straight knee strike to Fighter B's solar plexus area (another good target for the knee).

Insights

- Getting into a muay Thai clinch is usually done one hand at a time starting with the lead hand.

- To use knee strikes in the clinch, the opponent's head must be positioned below the fighter's head and at the center of the fighter's chest. This gives the fighter better control over the opponent as well as a clearer target.

- A fighter should never interlace his fingers when employing this clinch because it's more difficult for him to let go if he wants to.

- Tightening both forearms makes it more difficult for an adversary to escape and also constricts his blood flow, making him weaker.

- An opponent protects himself in the clinch by keeping his head raised and to the side of the fighter's chest.

- The best counter to escape the muay Thai clinch is by taking the opponent to the ground. However, this is easier said than done, as Anderson Silva's opponents know.

- Quick elbow strikes can be thrown by freeing one hand to perform the strike and quickly repositioning it in the clinch. This means that the fighter could lose the clinch, unless he's really quick.

Maneuvering the Opponent

1-3. With his arms tightly clamped around his opponent's neck, Fighter A can turn and steer Fighter B's head from the center and to the side. This way, he can execute a straight knee strike and an angular one without releasing his grip.

Additional Information
- ☞ dirty boxing clinch
- ☞ elbow strikes
- ☞ knee strikes
- ☞ wrestling clinch

NORTH/SOUTH POSITION

Description

This dominant top-fighting position places the competitors head-to-head and on the ground. The top fighter faces the ground, while the bottom fighter can be in the prone or supine position. The competitors' heads are pressed against each other's chest with their feet facing away and at opposite ends. As a hold-down position, the top fighter can use it to execute submission holds in which the *kimura* is the most common. The north/south position is also known as "front control" or the "69 position."

Applications
Transition to Kimura From North/South Position

1. During the dynamics of a match, Fighter A and Fighter B end up in the north/south position.

2. Fighter A grabs Fighter B's left wrist with his own left hand. He pins Fighter B's left arm to the ground in a downward "L" position (90-degree bend in the arm).

3. Next, Fighter A transitions from using his left hand to his right hand to securely pin his opponent's left arm at a 90-degree angle.

4. Once pinned, he immediately slides his left hand underneath Fighter B's upper arm.

5. Fighter A secures a figure-4 hold by grabbing his own right wrist with his left hand.

6. Once the figure-4 hold is secured, Fighter A immediately posts his left leg to the left of the opponent's head and pulls up on Fighter B's trapped left arm at the elbow.

7. The pull causes Fighter B's arm to raise his own left side up off the ground. Fighter A explosively rotates Fighter B's arm, driving his arm up in the direction toward his head. This causes him to tap in submission or risk a dislocated shoulder.

Insights

- Generally, the bottom opponent will be supine in the north/south position if the top opponent transitions from side control. He'll be prone if the top opponent transitions into a north/south position from a takedown.

- The top fighter is in a stable position unless the bottom opponent can find a way to reverse their positions.

Stable North/South Position

To maintain a stable north/south position, Fighter A spreads out his legs to base out his position. By balancing on the balls of his feet and pushing on his hips, Fighter A puts more pressure on Fighter B's head with his chest.

North/South Position With Knee Strikes

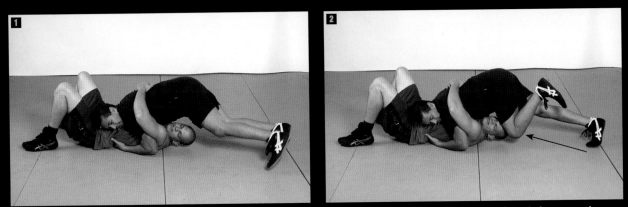

1-2. Fighter A lands a left straight knee strike to his opponent's head. Not many MMA organizations allow this technique nowadays.

Additional Information
- ☞ kimura
- ☞ side control

OMO PLATA

Description

The cousin of the *gogo plata*, the *omo plata* is a shoulder-lock submission hold in which a fighter traps the opponent's shoulder with his legs. By moving his hips forward, he cranks the shoulder, applying significant pressure that will force the opponent to submit. A fighter obtains the omo plata position by transitioning from the guard. If the fighter isn't on his back in a guard position, he won't be able to get in the right position to execute the move.

Application
Omo Plata From a Hip Sweep

1. Fighter A transitions from the closed guard into a crossover hip sweep. He hopes to reverse Fighter B.

2. Unfortunately, his attempt fails.

3. Fighter A immediately transitions into an omo plata by angling himself perpendicular to Fighter B. He swings his right leg over Fighter B's back.

4. From this position, he wraps his right leg around Fighter B's left arm, trapping it like a kimura but with his leg instead of his arm.

5. As he wraps his leg, Fighter A posts his left arm to sit up.

6. By posting and rotating his leg, Fighter A brings himself into a seated position.

Insights

- This is another submission hold that is pulled off from time to time. However, though it has shown its effectiveness, a fighter has to be fairly flexible and execute it with speed and precision because it can be easily countered if done otherwise.

- It's important to flatten out the opponent as soon as possible while applying this technique to prevent him from rolling out of it or pulling his arm out.

7. This seated position pins Fighter B's trapped arm so it is sandwiched between Fighter A's legs.

8-9. Fighter A slides his left leg to the outside, twisting Fighter B's arm like a pretzel. This cranks the shoulder.

10-11. To put even more pressure on Fighter B's shoulder, Fighter A grabs his head with both hands to pull up on it while raising his hips against Fighter B's bent and wedged left arm.

Additional Information
- ☞ crossover hip sweep
- ☞ gogo plata
- ☞ kimura

OPEN GUARD

Description

The open-guard position is the opposite of the closed-guard position; the fighter on the bottom has his legs open. A fighter uses the open guard to prevent his opponent from obtaining mount or side control while he transitions into a technique like a submission hold. Compared to the closed guard, the open guard is more flexible because it's easier to obtain submission holds, such as the armbar, arm triangle and *kimura,* for the bottom fighter. There are several variations to the open guard, ranging from keeping the legs/ankles uncrossed to keeping one or both feet on the opponent's hips or any variation in between.

Applications
Open Guard With One Foot on Hip

Fighter A keeps Fighter B from passing the guard by maintaining one foot on Fighter B's hip. This position also gives Fighter A the freedom to explosively transition into a submission hold.

Insight

- In conjunction with submission holds, a fighter can use the open guard to strike, grab, block or parry an opponent.

Open Guard With Both Feet on Hips

1-2. Using a transitional version of an open guard, Fighter A uses the position of his feet on both of Fighter B's hips to push him back. If enough space is created, Fighter A can do an up-kick to his opponent's chin as a good follow-up or transition into a submission hold.

Additional Information
- ☞ closed guard
- ☞ passing the guard
- ☞ top guard
- ☞ up-kick

OVERHAND (PUNCH)

Description

The overhand punch is a rear-hand power punch thrown in a convex arc (over the top) to the head. It is often used to go up and over an opponent's arm or as a simultaneous counterpunch over an opponent's jab. This punch is one of the four main power punches (along with the lead hook punch, rear hook punch and cross) in MMA.

Application
General Scenario for an Overhand Punch

1. Fighter A and Fighter B face off in matching orthodox stances.

2. When Fighter B fires off a left jab, Fighter A simultaneously counters with an overhand right.

Insights

- Generally, the overhand punch is executed with the rear hand because the lead overhand punch is too awkward and risky. The lead overhand punch leaves a fighter vulnerable to a possible takedown. However, that doesn't mean it isn't done. Fedor Emelianenko also throws this punch with his lead hand.

- While it is primarily used to go over an opponent's straight punch (be it left jab or right cross or vice versa), it can be used "down the line" or right down the middle, which is how Chuck Liddell throws it.

- It is an effective punch to use against a taller opponent to go over the top of his guard, especially as a counterattack.

- Like with any strike, proper punching form is a must. A fighter should keep his chin tucked down, hands up, elbows in and knees slightly bent. A fighter must also maintain good balance at all times. He should also always exhale upon execution and strike through the target.

3. The punch arches and goes over Fighter B's left arm, connecting with the left side of his jaw (ideally).

Additional Information
☞ cross (punch)
☞ hook (punch)
☞ jab (punch)
☞ uppercut (punch)

OVERHOOKS

Description

Overhooks are a wrestling-based move in which a fighter hooks one or both of his arms over and around one or both of his opponent's arms. Overhooks are very dynamic and employed in lots of scenarios. They are used to tie up, control and maneuver an opponent in a clinch. They are also used for transitioning into or thwarting a takedown. A competitor can also use overhooks in his ground game, such as tightly pulling an opponent in the guard.

Applications
Overhooks in a Clinch

Fighter A has overhooked his left arm with Fighter B's right arm in a clinch.

- Overhooks are a foundational part of the wrestling clinch.

- When a fighter thwarts a takedown with overhooks, he will usually apply a whizzer, too.

Takedown Counter

1. Fighter B attempts a body-lock takedown on Fighter A. Note that Fighter A has an overhook.

2. Fighter A thwarts the attempt with a left-arm overhook. He will then whizzer (whip) Fighter B to the right.

Additional Information
☞ body-lock takedowns
☞ whizzer
☞ wrestling clinch

PARRYING

Description

Parrying is used exclusively as a defensive measure against straight punches (jabs and crosses). Outside parries are safer to use than inside parries because they don't expose a fighter's head to an immediate follow-up shot by the opponent. To parry, a fighter uses the palm of his hand to deflect a punch to the inside or outside, depending on which hand he uses.

Applications
Parrying Straight Punches to the Outside

1. Fighter A and Fighter B face off in matching lead stances.

2. Fighter B launches a lead left jab, but Fighter A deflects with an outside parry.

3. When Fighter B attempts a rear right cross, Fighter A still stops it with an outside parry.

Insights

- A fighter usually blocks and covers to shield himself from attacks, but a parry deflects.
- Competitors can parry from any position, as long as they are both face-to-face.
- It is possible to redirect front kicks with a downward parry.

Risky Inside Parry

1. Fighter A and Fighter B face off in matching lead stances.

2. When Fighter B shoots out a lead left jab, Fighter A uses an inside parry to block it.

3. He pays the price for leaving his head exposed and unprotected because Fighter B follows up with a right cross to the jaw.

Additional Information

- ☞ covering
- ☞ cross (punch)
- ☞ front kick
- ☞ jab (punch)

PASSING THE GUARD

Description

Passing the guard refers to a fighter who escapes the closed or open guard by breaking free and going over or around the legs to obtain a mount, knee-on-stomach or side-control position. By passing the guard, the fighter takes away the opponent's power to control and manipulate him.

Applications
Passing the Closed Guard to Knee on Stomach

Closed

Open

1. In a top-guard position and wide-based standing posture, Fighter A pins both of Fighter B's arms to his chest. This prevents Fighter B from grabbing and pulling Fighter A in tight.

2-3. From here, Fighter A throws a straight left hand to Fighter B's face. The pain elicited from the punch causes his opponent to open up his closed guard.

4. The instant that he does, Fighter A thrusts his hips forward and arches his back, causing Fighter B's legs to rock backward.

5-6. As this is happening, Fighter A grabs Fighter B's right ankle with his left hand and throws Fighter B's legs off to the right.

7-8. This opens up his adversary's right side for Fighter A to assume a knee-on-belly position from which he can immediately ground-and-pound.

Insights

- There are hundreds of ways to pass the guard. For many fighters, passing the guard means breaking out of the opponent's legs and transitioning to side control, the mount or getting back to a free stand-up position to keep the fight upright.

- In the illustrations on page 137, Fighter A is able to open the guard by striking the inner thighs because he hits the sensitive femoral nerves in the legs.

Passing the Closed Guard to the Mount

1. While in a top-guard position inside the opponent's guard, Fighter A traps Fighter B's arms by grabbing his wrists and pinning them to his stomach. He also launches a left cross to Fighter B's face to distract him.

2. After punching him and maintaining the pin on Fighter B's arms, Fighter A immediately drives his elbows into Fighter B's inner thighs. This causes him to open his guard.

3-6. From here, Fighter A climbs over Fighter B's guard one knee at a time into the mount position. As soon as he establishes a solid mount, Fighter A blasts Fighter B with a left cross to the face.

Passing the Open Guard to Side Control

1. In the top position of an open guard, Fighter A traps Fighter B's hands by pinning them to his body.

2. From here, he punches Fighter B's face with a left cross and uses that "distraction" to immediately transition into breaking his adversary's guard.

3. Fighter A wedges his elbows into Fighter B's inner thighs, causing his opponent to open his guard.

4-7. This allows Fighter B to cross his right knee over Fighter B's guard and slide into side control.

Additional Information
- closed guard
- mount (position)
- knee on stomach
- open guard
- side control
- top guard

PERUVIAN NECKTIE

Description

The Peruvian necktie is a head-and-arm choke. The arms are positioned like the anaconda choke, but the legs are wrapped differently to stabilize the position and apply the choke. To execute the Peruvian necktie, the competitors must be in the north/south position with both fighters facing down. The fighter on top then executes the move.

Application
Double-Leg Takedown to Peruvian Necktie

1. Fighter B shoots in for a double-leg takedown, but Fighter A defends it with a sprawl.

2. By thwarting the sprawl, the two competitors end up on the ground in the north/south position with Fighter A on top. Fighter A brings his knees in close.

3. Like the anaconda choke, Fighter A applies a chokehold by maneuvering his left arm underneath Fighter B's neck and out through Fighter B's left armpit.

4. Upon doing so, Fighter A immediately grasps his left wrist with his right hand to lock the hold.

5. After securing this grip, Fighter A comes up with both feet, either one at a time or by jumping up with both at the same time. Fighter A also makes sure that his left foot is outside of Fighter B's right arm with the back of his left thigh over the right side of Fighter B's head. This move is crucial to the choke's success.

Insights

- While this choke is not as prevalently used as the rear-naked choke or the guillotine, I foresee it being applied more frequently as this move becomes better known. It is a fairly quick choke to secure and apply, with the one main drawback being that the positioning has to be just right for success.

- This choke was introduced and popularized in MMA competition by Tony DeSouza.

- It serves as UFC fighter C.B. Dollaway's favorite submission. He used it to submit Jesse Taylor at UFC: Silva vs. Irvin.

- Unlike the anaconda choke, the Peruvian necktie is technically a neck-cranking air choke because it cuts off airflow rather than blood flow.

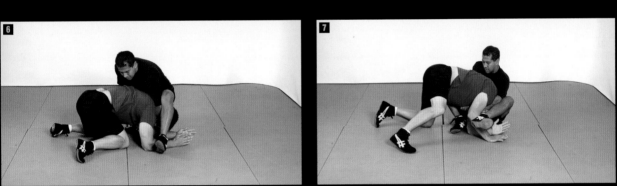

6-7. As soon as Fighter A is up on both feet, he sits back at roughly a 30- to 45-degree angle in relation to his opponent's position.

8-10. Right when Fighter A lands, he immediately drapes his right leg over his opponent's lower back. The draping of his right leg coupled with a hip-thrusting lean-back maneuver will apply torque to the neck and cause his opponent to submit or be rendered unconscious.

Additional Information
☞ anaconda choke
☞ guillotine choke
☞ rear-naked choke

PUMMELING

Description

Pummeling is a rapid-fire chess game in which two competitors scramble to get into a more dominant position while in a clinch. The wrestling tactic generally consists of both competitors maneuvering their arms to get past the other's lines of defense. Both fighters ultimately want to obtain underhooks in order to gain inside control of their opponent's body. Pummeling is an offensive and defensive maneuver done by both combatants at the same time. There are many different ways to execute this dynamic maneuver.

Application
Overhook/Underhook Pummeling

1-3. From a collar tie-up position, Fighter A pummels Fighter B, jockeying for inside control with overhooks an underhooks.

Insights

- Even though there are no specific positions for arms and legs, a fighter generally wants to keep his head and lead leg on the side of his overhooks until he obtains underhooks and a body-lock position.

- There is also neck-clinch pummeling in which one or both fighters are offensively and/or defensively maneuvering to obtain a *muay Thai* clinch or get out of one. The pummeling involved for muay Thai clinch is similar to overhook/underhook pummeling in that inside control is the objective sought to secure a tight two-handed clinch around an opponent's neck.

4. During the dynamic maneuver, Fighter A manages to get a handhold on Fighter B's body.

5. He takes control by bear-hugging Fighter B. He also transitions his head down to the center of Fighter B's chest for a takedown.

6. Fighter A pulls his hips in close to Fighter B's for a takedown.

Additional Information
☞ muay Thai clinch
☞ overhooks
☞ underhooks

PULLING GUARD

Description

This Brazilian *jiu-jitsu* term refers to a fighter who purposely puts an opponent inside his guard. The fighter conscientiously wants to put his opponent between his legs and control him from a supine ground position. It's most common to see a fighter pulling to the guard when both competitors are in a standing position.

Applications
Pulling Guard From the Clinch

1. Fighter A and Fighter B are in a clinch.

2. Fighter A proactively pulls Fighter B into his guard by jumping up and putting the guard around Fighter B's torso while both competitors are upright.

3. As he wraps his legs around Fighter B's waist, Fighter A pulls them both down, using his arms and legs.

4. This brings both competitors to the ground in a closed-guard position. Fighter A has the guard while Fighter B is in the guard. Fighter A also maintains the neck clinch to prevent Fighter B from escaping into a better position or striking.

Insights

- A fighter who "pulls guard" offensively is predominantly from a strong Brazilian jiu-jitsu background and is well-versed in executing submissions from this position. Now that most fighters know BJJ, it is generally not a recommended tactic unless the fighter's extremely confident working off his back. In sport BJJ, you can get away with this tactic more than in MMA because ground striking is not allowed.

- Generally speaking, "pulling guard" can be done defensively to prevent an opponent from obtaining a superior ground position (such as side control, the mount or back control).

- In the illustrations, the first sequence shows a fighter who is pulling to the guard proactively or offensively. The second sequence shows a fighter who is pulling to the guard reactively or defensively.

Pulling Guard From a Sprawl

1-2. Fighter B attempts a double-leg takedown, but Fighter A sprawls, taking him to the ground.

3-5. Fighter A reactively pulls Fighter B into the guard to prevent him from obtaining a more dominant ground position such as side control or the mount.

Additional Information
☞ sprawl

PUSH-AWAY/PUSH-DOWN TAKEDOWN DEFENSE

Description

When a fighter performs one of these techniques, he uses his hands and footwork to thwart the opponent's takedown attempt. The push-away defense, as the name implies, pushes the opponent away. The push-down defense involves redirecting the opponent's forward movement by driving him to the ground. This is the basic, first-line defensive technique against any kind of takedown attempt.

Applications
Push-Away Defense

1. From an unmatched lead, Fighter A and Fighter B face off.

2. Fighter B shoots in for a double-leg takedown, and Fighter A immediately responds by reaching out his hands. He places them on Fighter B's head and shoulders to push his opponent away and to keep Fighter B from grabbing at his legs.

3. As he does this, Fighter A simultaneously uses circling footwork to step off to the side.

4. Because Fighter B is still pushing himself forward for the takedown, the defense causes him to follow through and fall down into open space.

Insights

- When doing these defenses, a fighter uses circling footwork, which helps him move quickly and efficiently in a circle.

- Hand placement and timing are crucial to each application's success. Both hands are generally placed along an opponent's head, neck, shoulder and upper-arm areas in any combination that fits the moment. These are ideal areas that prevent the opponent from grabbing the fighter and pushing him away.

- The actual push-away must be combined with the use of circling footwork, which can either be in a clockwise or counterclockwise direction. If the fighter is on the opponent's right side, then he should circle clockwise. If the fighter is on the opponent's left side (the left side of his head and shoulder area), he should circle counterclockwise.

Push-Down Defense

1. Fighter A and Fighter B are in unmatched stances.

2. Fighter B shoots in for a double-leg takedown, which Fighter A thwarts by stepping back and placing one hand on Fighter B's head and the other on Fighter B's shoulder.

3. With his hands in place, Fighter A pushes Fighter B straight to the ground, putting him in a prone position

4. After doing so, Fighter A immediately circles counterclockwise and returns to an upright fighting stance.

Additional Information
☞ double-leg takedown

QUARTER NELSON

Description

The quarter nelson is a wrestling-based maneuver used to counter takedown attempts, especially single-leg takedowns. A fighter uses a figure-4 hold around the opponent's head/neck to apply pressure against the grasping arm or to break the grip.

Application
General Quarter-Nelson Scenario

1. Fighter B attempts a single-leg takedown.

2. Fighter A immediately tries to get out of it by putting his trapped leg to the outside.

3. He applies a quarter nelson. He overhooks Fighter B's left armpit and places his left hand on top of Fighter B's head. He grabs his left wrist with his right hand, trapping Fighter B's arm in a figure-4 hold.

4. Here, Fighter A executes the technique by pushing down on Fighter B's head and pulling up on Fighter B's armpit. Fighter A also kicks back his raised leg, creating a push-pull action that frees it.

Insights

- Even though competitors generally thwart a double-leg takedown with a cross-face, it's also possible to do it with a quarter nelson.

- A fighter can transition to a whizzer from a quarter nelson once the opponent's hold around his leg is broken.

5. The quarter nelson also breaks Fighter B's balance and brings him to the ground, while Fighter A is left free to disengage and counterattack from a standing position or on the ground.

Additional Information
☞ cross-face
☞ figure-4 hold
☞ whizzer

REAR-NAKED CHOKE

Description

The rear-naked choke is the premier choking technique in MMA as well as one of the most effective and frequently used submissions, alongside the guillotine choke, triangle choke, armbar and *kimura*. It is a choke used when a fighter is behind the opponent in back control. A fighter encircles one of his arms tightly around the opponent's neck and uses his other arm to tightly secure the hold. From there, a fighter forces a submission or renders the opponent unconscious by squeezing the encircled arm at the elbow's crook. The rear-naked choke is a versatile blood choke that can be applied from a variety of positions—including standing, sitting, kneeling, on one's hands and knees, supine or prone—and any position in which you can establish back control.

Applications
Rear-Naked Choke Applied From a Prone Position

1-2. From a back-control position, Fighter A does a double-grapevine maneuver on Fighter B's legs to break him down—stretch him out—to a flat prone position.

3. From here, Fighter A immediately encircles his left arm around Fighter B's neck, meaning the crook of his elbow is in line with Fighter B's throat. Fighter A also places his left hand on Fighter B's right biceps.

4. Fighter A takes his right hand and places it behind Fighter B's head. He tucks his own head over Fighter B's right shoulder and keeps his eyes closed to defend against eye-gouge attempts.

5. Once this figure-4 position around his neck is secured, Fighter A applies pressure to Fighter B's neck by squeezing and closing the "V" at the crook of his left elbow. He also presses his chest down, simultaneously exhaling. With this pressure, Fighter B will either tap or be rendered unconscious within three to 10 seconds.

Insights

- The rear-naked choke is also known as the RNC or *mata leon,* which in Portuguese means "lion kill."

- The choke can actually be applied as a blood or air choke depending on the position of the choking arm. Generally, it is more often applied as a blood choke that targets the carotid arteries.

- It usually takes three to 10 seconds to render an opponent unconscious. If a fighter keeps it on for more than 30 seconds, he risks causing brain damage or death to his opponent.

- If a person could only choose one choke to master and functionalize, it should be this one.

- In terms of how to get out of it, the best way is to not get into it in the first place. If the opponent does get his choking arm around the fighter's neck, the fighter has to get it off his neck with two-handed control and put his opponent's arm over the fighter's opposite shoulder. (Meaning, if the opponent is using his right arm as his choking arm, once the fighter controls it and gets it off from around his neck, he has to put it over his left shoulder.) Both of these counter-maneuvers are not shown.

- While not clearly shown, it is important to encircle the choking arm around the opponent's neck, like a boa constrictor would do it. Slide/slither the choking arm around the neck, keeping constant contact rather than using a wide, looping movement to do it. Doing the latter allows the opponent to counter it more easily.

Rear-Naked Choke Applied From a Supine Position

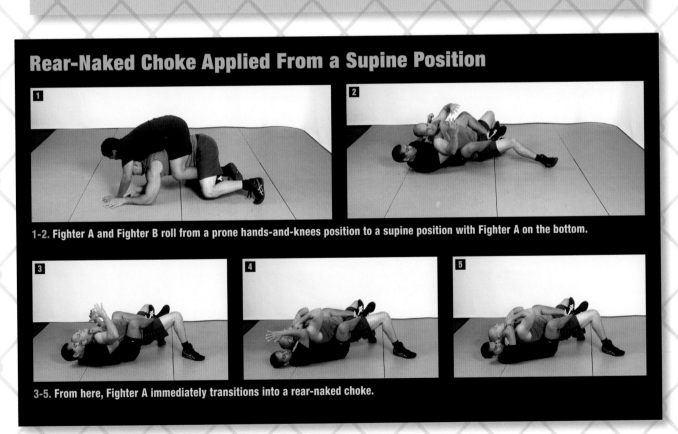

1-2. Fighter A and Fighter B roll from a prone hands-and-knees position to a supine position with Fighter A on the bottom.

3-5. From here, Fighter A immediately transitions into a rear-naked choke.

Additional Information
- ☞ armbar
- ☞ guillotine choke
- ☞ kimura
- ☞ triangle choke

ROUND KICK

Description

The round kick is the most effective and utilized kick in MMA. It is an inward circular kick that travels outside in a horizontal or diagonal trajectory. The kick uses the shin or instep to strike at an opponent's head, body or legs; the body targets are specifically the ribs, liver or spleen. It is the trademark technique of *muay Thai* and is responsible for a majority of the head-kick knockouts produced in MMA. The round kick is the muay Thai and MMA term used for the roundhouse. When directed to the thighs, it is also referred to as a leg kick.

Applications
Round Kick to the Leg

1. From matching lead fighting stances, Fighter A prepares to step off to the right with his foot at a 45-degree angle. This opens up his hips for the kick.

2. Whipping back his left arm and circling right, Fighter A creates a synergistic movement that adds torque to the kick.

3. Fighter A whips his rear leg in a horizontal trajectory to Fighter B's outer thigh. He will then retract the kick to his original fighter stance. Note: If he missed his target, Fighter A would set his kicking leg down in front or spin all the way around, muay Thai style, back to his fighting stance.

Round Kick to the Inner Thigh

From unmatched lead fighting stances, Fighter A lands a left round kick to Fighter B's inner thigh. The body mechanics are exactly the same as shown in the first example.

Insights

- The main round-kick targets are the outer and inner thigh/sciatic nerve, the rib-cage or liver area on the right side of an opponent's body, the rib-cage or spleen area on the left side of an opponent's body, and the head, specifically the jaw or temple areas. All can take out an opponent, the first two via TKO by pain and the last by pure KO.

- The lead leg has utility, as well, and it is used with greater frequency by such MMA standouts as Georges St. Pierre and Cung Le. Even though it is not known to have the same power as the rear leg, with proper timing and accuracy, it can produce a knockout, too. (See Georges St. Pierre's round kick TKO of Matt Hughes at UFC 65: Bad Intentions.)

- As alluded to in the photo sequences, the key to generating power is to initiate momentum with the 45-degree-angled outside step along with the ensuing hip whip and a short, sharp exhalation.

- When it comes to leg kicks, don't be deceived by the sound when it connects with an opponent's thigh. The hardest kicks are actually the ones that land with a dull thud with not much sound behind it. That means the leg kick is penetrating down to the bone as opposed to the leg kick that elicits a loud slapping sound. The latter kick is indicative of contact made by the instep with not much penetration.

- As indicated, it's possible to do round kicks from standing or ground position. If a fighter is on the ground, he can only do a round kick if he is on his back in the shell position.

Round Kick With the Lead Leg

1-3. In this sequence, Fighter A does a shuffle step, bringing his left foot up next to his right foot. This closes the distance and generates momentum for the kick. He executes a right round kick, targeting his opponent's left outer thigh with his right instep. While shooting out the kick, Fighter A simultaneously "whips" his lead arm back with a "push-pull" energy to increase the torque of the kicking action.

Round Kick to the Head

Fighter A lands a left round kick with his instep to the right side of Fighter B's head, hitting his jaw in the process. This is the ideal target and round kick variation to KO an opponent.

Additional Information
☞ shell position

RUBBER GUARD

Description

The rubber guard is a relatively recent guard variation developed by Brazilian *jiu-jitsu* instructor Eddie Bravo. It's also being used with more and more frequency in MMA competitions. The guard consists of adopting a high guard with one leg that goes around the back of an opponent's neck and is secured with one or both hands. The objective is to pull the opponent down into a tightly clinched position in which the fighter can transition into submission holds such as a triangle choke, *omo plata* or *gogo plata*.

Application
General Rubber-Guard Scenario

1. From a closed-guard position with his right hand secured around his opponent's neck, Fighter A uncrosses his legs and posts his right foot against Fighter B's right hip for leverage.

2. While doing this, Fighter A climbs his left leg up Fighter B's back.

3. He pulls Fighter B closer with his hands to bring his rival in close to apply the rubber guard.

4. With the opponent secured, Fighter A continues inching his left leg up, and as soon as he can, he grabs his left ankle with his right hand.

Insights

- From either mission or retard control, a fighter can maneuver into a number of different positions to transition into submission holds like the omo plata, gogo plata, triangle choke or armbar.

- The rubber guard is the brainchild of Bravo, a Hollywood, California, Brazilian jiu-jitsu instructor who earned his black belt from renowned BJJ instructor Jean Jacques Machado. The rubber guard has invaded MMA competition because of its functionality in the sport. It is a good guard to break down and control an opponent with.

- Having said that, there is one caveat worth mentioning: Fighters need to have fairly flexible hips and legs to learn and functionally apply the maneuver in competition. So if a fighter is not flexible, this move most likely won't work.

5. He cinches the rubber guard by squeezing his leg and arm together, which pulls Fighter B's head down in the process. This particular position is known as "mission control."

6. Fighter A transitions from "mission control" into "retard control" by clasping his hands together on top of his left ankle for even tighter control.

Additional Information

☞ armbar
☞ gogo plata
☞ omo plata
☞ triangle choke

SCARF HOLD

Description

The scarf hold is a side-control position that is characterized by one arm around the supine opponent's head and the other controlling the opponent's right or left arm, depending on his position. The fighter's legs are based out wide. The position allows the dominant fighter to apply pressure to his adversary by pressing his chest down with his own chest or via head-lock pressure. The fighter on top is then in a good position to transition into submission holds like an Americana or arm triangle.

Applications
Basic Scarf Hold

Overhooking Fighter B's right arm with his left, Fighter A holds him in a scarf hold with his legs based out wide. Fighter A secures the position by squeezing Fighter B's neck tightly with his right arm. He reinforces his side-control position by exerting downward body pressure on Fighter B's chest with his own chest. He wants to restrict and constrict Fighter B as much as possible.

Insight

- To solidly establish and maintain this position, a fighter shouldn't overextend his body weight over the center of the opponent's chest but instead keep pressure on the opponent's side. Overextension allows the opponent to reverse position by rolling the fighter over his own body and into a complementary side-control position with the opponent on top.

Reinforced Scarf Hold

Fighter A reinforces his scarf hold by grasping his own thigh with his right hand to lock Fighter B in place.

Additional Information
- ☞ scarf-hold Americana
- ☞ arm triangle
- ☞ side control

SCARF-HOLD AMERICANA

Description

This is a variation of the figure-4 Americana in that the shoulder lock is applied from the scarf-hold position. Otherwise, it is still a submission hold that traps the wrist and cranks the shoulder with a distinguishing upward L-shape.

Application
General Scarf-Hold Americana Scenario

1. From side control, Fighter A transitions into a scarf hold by sliding his right leg underneath Fighter B's right arm.

2. Once in the scarf hold, Fighter A immediately grabs Fighter B's exposed right wrist and pushes it down to the ground.

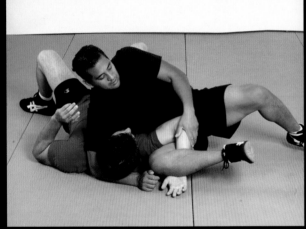

3. When the opponent's arm hits the mat, Fighter A pins it by sliding his right leg over Fighter B's right arm, which is bent at a 90-degree L-shape position.

4. He secures the trapped arm by hooking his own foot underneath the crook of his left knee.

Insight

- Besides the Americana, the scarf hold is a good position to apply other submission holds such as the arm triangle and a step-over armbar.

5. From here, Fighter A cranks the Americana by lifting Fighter B's head off the ground while keeping his armed pinned in a figure-4 hold on the ground.

Additional Information
- ☞ Americana
- ☞ omo plata
- ☞ scarf hold

SCISSOR SWEEP

Description

    This sweep is a fundamental Brazilian *jiu-jitsu* guard-reversal technique. The defensive maneuver uses a scissoring leg action, which gives a fighter in the bottom-guard position the proper leverage to reverse himself into a dominant mount position. Leg positioning is important in this technique.

Application
General Scissor-Sweep Scenario

1. While in Fighter A's closed guard, Fighter B throws an overhand right to the head.

2. Fighter A blocks it and immediately uncrosses his legs to plant his feet on the ground.

3. Fighter A also secures a hold around the back of Fighter B's neck and maintains a grip on Fighter B's right arm.

4. By shrimping, Fighter A maneuvers onto his left side, positioning his legs like scissors. His left leg is on the ground and presses Fighter B's shin. His right leg is positioned across Fighter B's torso with his right instep pressed against Fighter B's rib cage.

Insights

- An opponent can nullify the scissor sweep by lying down on top of the attacking fighter's upper leg. This is why the fighter wants to keep his top-positioned leg on the opponent's solar plexus or upper chest.

- On that note, the lower leg must be lying flat on the ground pressed against the opponent's knee/shin area. If a fighter's bottom leg is raised off the deck, the scissoring action takes more strength to complete.

- There are many variations of the scissor sweep, like the half-butterfly elevator sweep.

Additional Information

☞ crossover hip sweep
☞ half-butterfly elevator sweep

5. He displaces his opponent's center of gravity, using his legs to scissor-sweep Fighter B to the ground. His "top" leg kicks forward, and his "bottom" leg kicks back. Fighter A simultaneously pushes and pulls Fighter B's arms with his hands to augment the sweep.

6. This combined leg-scissoring and arm pushing-pulling action results in "sweeping" the opponent from a top-guard position and reversing him into a bottom position.

7-8. As soon as he's in the mount, Fighter A grounds-and-pounds Fighter B with alternating straight punches to the face.

SHELL POSITION

Description

This defensive supine position is like a protective shell against a standing opponent. A fighter who is on his back uses it as a platform to protect himself from kicks, punches or other attempts by the standing opponent to gain a dominant ground-fighting position. To establish a shell position, a fighter draws in his arms and knees, forming his body into a tight shell. From that position, he can execute an up-kick, stomp kick or round kick.

Application
General Shell-Position Scenario

1. With Fighter B standing over him, Fighter A defends himself in a shell position. Note how his arms and legs are bent, tucked in and drawn to his body.

2. Fighter B still attempts to launch a straight punch, like the cross, at Fighter A.

Insights

- No matter what position a fighter is in, it's vitally important that he face his opponent whenever possible in order to protect his head.

- The best counter to a shell position is to kick the ground fighter in the legs, punch him in the face, or push his legs to the side to get side-control, knee-on-belly or another dominant position.

- A fighter in the shell position doesn't want to stay grounded too long. His main goal is to stand up quickly.

- An excellent way to regain a standing position from the shell position is the standing-up-in base maneuver from Brazilian *jiu-jitsu*.

3. To defend himself, Fighter A shoots an up-kick to Fighter B's face.

4. He then lands a left round kick to Fighter B's left inner thigh.

Additional Information
- 🖝 round kick
- 🖝 standing up in base
- 🖝 stomp kick
- 🖝 up-kick

SHOULDER BUTT

Description

The shoulder butt is an offensive strike that is applied by thrusting either shoulder in the opponent's face. It's a close-range strike that a fighter uses to distract an adversary, keep him on the defensive and create an opening. The shoulder butt can be executed from a clinch position, the mount or side control. When on the ground, a fighter drops his shoulder to apply it. If both competitors are standing, the fighter drives his shoulder upward to apply the strike.

Applications
Shoulder Butt From the Mount

1-2. While in the mount, Fighter A executes a left shoulder butt by dropping his left shoulder into Fighter B's face.

Shoulder Butt From Side Control

1-2. While in side control, Fighter A executes a left shoulder butt by dropping his left shoulder into Fighter B's face.

Insights

- While this strike won't knock an opponent out, it is a good distraction shot to set up a more potent offensive attack.

- Because the strike is based on surprise and opportunity, there's really no way to counter it specifically. Generally, a competitor will keep his head and body in tight to avoid strikes anyway.

Shoulder Butt From Clinch

1-2. Fighter A executes a right shoulder butt to Fighter B's face by thrusting it upward with a augmenting push-off from his rear foot.

Additional Information
☞ dirty boxing clinch
☞ mount
☞ muay Thai clinch
☞ side control
☞ wrestling clinch

SIDE CONTROL

Description

Side control is a dominant offensive ground position in which the fighter lies on his side on top of a supine opponent. Both competitors are, in a sense, chest-to-chest. This versatile position is used to control bottom opponents and to execute a myriad of submission holds. A fighter also uses it as a stable platform to ground-and-pound. Side control is also known as the "cross body" or "cross side" position.

Applications
Ideal Side-Control Position

Fighter A is in side control with both knees drawn in against Fighter B. This adaptation is widely considered to be the best position to adopt in side control because it is the most secure and versatile platform to ground-and-pound or transition into a submission hold from.

Based-Out Side Control

Fighter A is in side control with both legs splayed out in a wide stable base. This is a good position to temporarily pin down an opponent and transition into a scarf-hold position because it's easier for Fighter A to spread out his legs to scarf.

Insights

- Establishing a good side-control position revolves around the Brazilian *jiu-jitsu* maxim "contact equals control, space equals escape." It's crucial for a fighter to have chest-to-chest contact and his arms wrapped around the opponent very tightly, inhibiting the opponent's ability to maneuver his hips to create space.

- Tighter contact can also be applied by exerting downward/inward hip pressure.

- Many fighters find the side-control position a more advantageous offensive position than the mount in that they can ground-and-pound with more techniques, such as knees, and are in a better position to transition into submission holds.

- It's also easier to stand back up from side control, if the top fighter so chooses.

- Side control is sometimes called side mount, but it's not to be confused with the side-mount entry.

Side Control With a Posted Leg

Fighter A is in side control with his left knee drawn in to Fighter B's hip and his right leg posted out. This side-control position is applied to block an opponent who is trying to apply a side-escape maneuver to place the fighter in his guard; Fighter A knee blocks Fighter B's leg so his opponent can't turn into him.

Additional Information
☞ scarf hold
☞ side mount

SIDE KICK

Description

The side kick is a sideward, lateral kick that is most often executed with the lead leg. It generally targets an opponent's midsection in MMA competition.

Application
General Side-Kick Scenario

1. Fighter A and Fighter B face off in matching leads.

2. Fighter A slides his rear foot to the position of his lead foot, and as soon as they touch, he chambers his lead knee.

Insights

- While not employed as frequently as its more prolific and effective cousin the round kick, the side kick has shown its worth through renowned fighters such as Lyoto Machida, Georges St. Pierre and Cung Le.

- One reason this kick is not used as much as the round or front is because the fighter's side is exposed. It's much easier to employ techniques from a more front-facing position, and many MMA fighters find it awkward to follow up a side kick with other offensive techniques.

- Defensively, the side kick is good to use to keep an opponent at bay and prevent him from closing the gap.

- A side kick is a good transition kick to use after a missed rear round kick to the leg.

3. He follows the chamber by thrusting his left foot out in a straight, lateral line at Fighter B's stomach.

Additional Information
☞ front kick
☞ round kick

SIDE MOUNT

Description

This is a modified mount position in which one of the top fighter's knees is up and the other is down. It is employed when the supine opponent turns to one side as he's trying to roll over. If the opponent's on his left side, the fighter's right foot is posted. If the opponent's on his right side, the fighter's left foot is posted.

Application
Ground and Pound From Side Mount

1. From the mount position, Fighter A arm-wraps Fighter B's right arm.

2. With the arm wrap secured, Fighter A pushes Fighter B's right elbow and pulls Fighter B's right wrist, turning his body to the left.

3. While doing this, Fighter A transitions from the mount into the side mount. He makes sure to post his right foot and slide his left knee up against Fighter B's back to keep close contact.

4. This tight contact with the legs and tight wrapping of the neck keeps Fighter B on his side.

Insights

- Generally, a fighter will achieve side mount not on purpose but because the opponent is trying to turn.

- Besides being in a good position to ground-and-pound an opponent, the side mount is also a good technique to transition into an armbar submission and a variety of chokes.

- Often, people will refer to the side mount as the mount position. But technically, the position is very different because of the position of the legs along with the opponent being on his side.

5. From this position, Fighter A grounds-and-pounds Fighter B with right-handed punches and elbows.

Additional Information
☞ armbar
☞ arm wrap
☞ mount

SINGLE-LEG TAKEDOWN

Description

This is a major, bread-and-butter takedown derived from wrestling. A fighter shoots in and goes after a single leg to immobilize it, control it, and use it to off-balance and take down the opponent. There are numerous ways to do a single-leg takedown with inside and outside trips, spin trips, or throwing the leg up to put him down.

Applications
Single-Leg Takedown by Closing the Gap

1. From unmatched leads, Fighter A sets up a basic single-leg takedown with a right jab to distract Fighter B.

2. Immediately after executing the jab, Fighter A shoots in to close the gap between him and Fighter B.

3. He captures Fighter B's lead left leg by hooking it with his lead right arm. To secure the hold, Fighter A does a hand-to-wrist clasp.

4. From there, Fighter A lifts Fighter B's left leg up and simultaneously drives his own right shoulder into Fighter B's left hip, applying downward pressure.

5. By driving forward with a penetrating step, Fighter A accentuates the downward pressure, taking Fighter B to the ground.

6. Once grounded, Fighter A immediately maneuvers into a left side-control position.

Insights

- It's not as potent a takedown as the double-leg takedown, but it has its uses and is a good alternative to transition to when a double-leg shot is thwarted.

- Nowadays, this takedown is most often applied in transitions from a body-lock position, especially when pressed up against a cage, because competitors are too familiar with a sprawl defense.

Single-Leg Takedown From the Clinch

1. From a tie-up clinch position, Fighter A and Fighter B jockey for position.

2. Fighter A quickly circles clockwise and suddenly drops into a semi-crouch position, immediately snatching Fighter B's left leg with his right arm.

3. To secure his hold, Fighter B uses a hand-to-wrist clasp. From there, he raises Fighter B's leg up and simultaneously drives his own right shoulder into Fighter B's left hip, applying downward pressure.

4. To accentuate the pressure, Fighter A takes a penetration step forward, driving Fighter B to the ground.

5. Once grounded, Fighter A quickly transitions into a left side-control position.

Additional Information
☞ double-leg takedown
☞ sprawl

SLIPPING

Description

Slipping describes a common evasive maneuver that face-to-face competitors will use on the ground or while standing. A fighter moves his head laterally to the inside or outside of an opponent's straight punches to evade them.

Applications
Outside Slips

1. Fighter A and Fighter B face each other in matching orthodox stances.

2. When Fighter B launches a left jab, Fighter A slips to the right by moving his head just enough for the strike to miss. He slips to the outside of the punch.

3. When Fighter B follows up with a left cross, Fighter A is still able to avoid the strike by slipping. He still slips to the outside of the punch.

Insights

- A fighter can slip to the inside or outside of an opponent's straight punch. However, it's more prudent to use outside slips because they are safer. Inside slips bring a fighter's head directly in line with the opponent's other hand.

- Slips should be as economical as possible, only moving the head enough for the punch to barely miss. The reason is that it allows a fighter to position himself to counter quicker.

Inside Slips

1-3. From matching stances, Fighter A executes a right inside slip against his opponent's right jab. However (and this is the danger with using inside slips), Fighter B nails Fighter A on the chin with an immediate follow-up left cross.

Additional Information
☞ cross (punch)
☞ jab (punch)

SPINNING BACKFIST

Description

The spinning backfist is a hand technique based on surprise and opportunity. A fighter spins around 180 degrees to throw a whipping follow-through backfist strike to the opponent's head. If applied correctly, it is a knockout punch.

Application
General Spinning-Backfist Scenario

1. From unmatched leads, Fighter A and Fighter B face off.

2. Fighter A steps to his left with his lead right foot to facilitate the spinning motion that will propel the strike.

Insights

- This is infrequently used because, more often than not, it doesn't land and leaves the fighter vulnerable to counters of all varieties.

- The technique was made famous when Shonie Carter won by TKO over Matt Serra in the UFC 31.

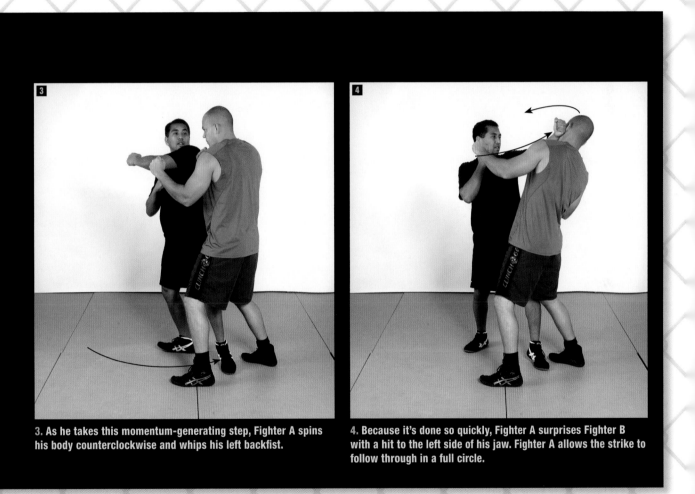

3. As he takes this momentum-generating step, Fighter A spins his body counterclockwise and whips his left backfist.

4. Because it's done so quickly, Fighter A surprises Fighter B with a hit to the left side of his jaw. Fighter A allows the strike to follow through in a full circle.

Additional Information
☞ spinning back kick

SPINNING BACK KICK

Description

This kick is only occasionally used because it is based on surprise and opportunity. A fighter spins around in 180 degrees to throw a back kick straight into an opponent's midsection. The purpose of the kick is to knock the wind out of the opponent or break one of his ribs.

Application
General Spinning Back-Kick Scenario

1. Fighter A is squared off against Fighter B in unmatched leads.

2. Fighter A pivots his feet, twists his body and turns his head to the left, counterclockwise.

Insights

- Even though infrequently used, the spinning back kick packs a wallop and can even take out an opponent if it solidly lands. There have been enough instances in which this has occurred that many fighters include it in their arsenal.

- Recently, Cung Le and others have applied this kick effectively.

3-5. With his back momentarily facing Fighter B, Fighter A uses the momentum generated by the spinning motion to execute a back kick off of his left foot and straight to and through Fighter B's midsection.

Additional Information
☞ spinning backfist

SPRAWL

Description

This is the No. 1 move to thwart any takedown maneuver. Derived from wrestling, a sprawl counters a lower-body takedown attempt such as the oft-used double-leg takedown. A fighter executes a sprawl when he throws his legs back and applies downward pressure with his hips. He simultaneously spreads his legs wide apart to thwart the opponent's attempt at securely grasping one or both of his legs for a takedown. Coupled with a cross-face, underhooks, overhooks, a quarter nelson or a simple head push-down, a sprawl puts a fighter in a good position to break free, stand up again or transition to a more advantageous ground-fighting position.

Application
Sprawl With a Cross-Face and Quarter Nelson

1. From matching leads, Fighter B throws a jab to distract Fighter A and set up a takedown attempt.

2. Immediately after putting a jab in Fighter A's face, Fighter B shoots in with a double-leg takedown.

3. Fighter A thwarts it by shooting his own legs back and thrusting his hips down and forward to apply pressure against Fighter B's right shoulder and the grasp around his legs. In addition to this, Fighter A simultaneously spreads his legs apart widely while shooting them back explosively.

4. In conjunction to all that, Fighter A pushes down on Fighter B's neck with his right hand and underhooks Fighter B's right arm with his left arm to further prevent a good hold of his legs. He maintains his downward pressure throughout the entire technique.

5. Fighter A applies a cross-face to exert pressure against Fighter B's head/neck area in the opposite direction he's applying his. This compounds the pressure Fighter A is applying to Fighter B's arms and right shoulder area with his hips.

Insights

- This is undisputedly the primary takedown defense maneuver to master.

- It is the foundational move to thwart any lower-body takedowns.

- Anytime a fighter sprawls, he needs to do something with his upper body. Aside from the cross-face and quarter nelson, a fighter can also apply such techniques as the whizzer, double underhook, an underhook-overhook combo, etc.

6. To break his opponent's hold even more, Fighter A transitions into a quarter nelson.

7. Here, Fighter A applies a quarter nelson with an overhook and by applying his hand to the back of Fighter B's head for downward pressure.

8. This breaks Fighter B's hold, allowing Fighter A to circle clockwise to obtain back control.

9. Fighter A succeeds in getting a top-turtle back-mount position.

Additional Information
- ☞ cross-face
- ☞ double-leg takedown
- ☞ quarter nelson
- ☞ turtle position
- ☞ whizzer

SPRAWL AND BRAWL

Description

Like the ground and pound, the sprawl and brawl is a core MMA fighting tactic, but it is executed while standing rather than on the ground. A fighter who prefers to fight standing uses it in order to thwart takedowns, avoid ground fighting and keep the fight in an upright position.

Application
General Sprawl-and-Brawl Scenario

1. From unmatched stances, Fighter B shoots in with a double-leg takedown.

2. Fighter A defends against it with a sprawl.

3. Immediately after thwarting his takedown attempt, Fighter A disengages, breaking free.

Insights

- A good sprawl-and-brawler adapts his overall game to revolve around takedown and ground-fighting counters/defenses.

- Chuck Liddell, Wanderlei Silva and Mirko "Cro Cop" Filopovic are three of the most renowned sprawl-and-brawl exponents in MMA.

4-7. Fighter A follows up by brawling with uppercuts, overhands and round kicks to Fighter B's face and body.

Additional Information
☞ sprawl

Description

This fundamental starting position serves as the primary stand-up fighting platform. It is the on-guard position from which to employ standing offense and defense from. There are basically two types of stances utilized in MMA, an upright on-guard stance and a semi-crouched stance. An upright stance is basically the platform for stand-up fighting, while a semi-crouched stance is a platform to shoot in on an opponent to take him down and for thwarting/countering takedown attempts. Both stances can also be used deceptively and interchangeably to set up strikes and takedowns.

Applications
Standard Upright On-Guard Stance

1. Fighter A stands with his shoulders slightly hunched, chin tucked in, elbows tucked in, knees slightly bent and hands up by his jaw. His feet are roughly shoulder-width apart with the lead foot pointing straight ahead, turned very slightly inward, with the rear foot slightly raised on the ball of his foot and at a 45-degree angle. The weight distribution is 50-50.

2. Fighter A is in the standard upright on-guard stance but with his lead hand slightly lower and held a little more out in front of him. This has become a common variation of the upright stance.

Insights

- Stances are not precise, exact positions but rather individualistic fighting platforms that should be tailored according to a fighter's build and predilections.

- Like with punches, stances also must be based on sound, fundamental guidelines such as keeping the chin down, shoulders slightly hunched, elbows tucked in, hands up, knees bent, feet roughly shoulder-width apart and weight distributed 50-50.

- These positions are used throughout the entire book.

Standard Semi-Crouched Stance

Fighter A stands in a semi-crouched fighting stance with basically the same characteristics as the upright stance except that his knees are more pronouncedly bent and his upper body is leaning forward a bit more.

Additional Information

- ☞ cross (punch)
- ☞ hook (punch)
- ☞ jab (punch)
- ☞ overhand (punch)
- ☞ uppercut (punch)

STANDING UP IN BASE

Description

This Brazilian *jiu-jitsu* derived maneuver helps a fighter get back up to his feet from a shell position. In this tactic, "base" refers to stance; it's just the more commonly applied term in BJJ.

Application
General Standing-Up-in-Base Scenario

1. Fighter A is in a shell position when Fighter B attempts to close the gap and strike him.

2. He turns to his left and posts his left hand slightly behind him.

3. Fighter A immediately raises his right foot as a protective barrier and shoots out a right stomp kick to keep Fighter B at bay.

4. As soon as Fighter B takes a step backward, Fighter A sets his right foot down and immediately pushes off it to drive himself backward and away from his opponent.

Insights

- This move is a fundamentally important one that is often not practiced enough.

- It is a safe and excellent maneuver for standing back up from a shell position.

5. As space is created between the two competitors, Fighter A slides his left leg out from underneath him and posts it behind him, obtaining an upright position.

6. Fighter A keeps his right arm out as a barrier. Upon gaining a standing position, Fighter A immediately adopts his fighting stance and proceeds from there.

Additional Information
☞ shell position

STOMP KICK

Description

The stomp kick is a straight thrusting kick executed from a supine ground position against a standing opponent. It is launched at an angle, targeting the approaching adversary's stomach. The main purpose of the stomp kick is to keep the standing opponent on the defensive so the grounded fighter can stand up. It is also known as the "thrust kick."

Application
General Stomp-Kick Scenario

1. Fighter A lands a right stomp kick to Fighter B's midsection that bends him at the waist.

Insight

- Coupled with the up-kick and round kick, the stomp kick is a good one to use from the ground against an upright opponent looking to kick the grounded fighter's legs, "dive" in with an overhand punch or engage in a ground fight. Besides the aforementioned, it is also used to drive back an opponent, giving the grounded fighter the opportunity to stand up in base.

Additional Information

- ☞ round kick
- ☞ standing up in base
- ☞ up-kick

2. He follows up with a left stomp kick to Fighter B's right thigh, which displaces it and puts Fighter B off-balance.

SUPERMAN PUNCH

Description

The superman punch is like a superpower cross. It is a powerful, leaping rear-hand straight punch deceptively thrown off of a distracting knee chamber. The knee movement also charges up the punch, making it a knockout strike.

Applications
General Superman-Punch Scenario

1. Fighter A fakes a left leg front kick. The movement lets him chamber his left knee.

2. Immediately, Fighter A pushes off his right leg, explosively leaping up.

3. In a whiplike fashion, he chambers his left hand like a slingshot and blasts Fighter B with a powerful straight punch to the jaw.

Insights

- While this punch can be looked on as telegraphic, there have been a good many knockouts that have resulted from it. The most prominent use of the punch was in UFC Fight Night: Kenny Florian vs. Joe Lauzon in which James Irvin scored a KO over Houston Alexander in eight seconds.

- Georges St. Pierre uses this punch effectively off of both the rear and lead hand sides.

Exaggerated Superman

1-3. This sequence shows an exaggerated version of the superman punch in an attempt to convey the leaping whiplike motion in the shot and the powerful torque this motion generates.

Additional Information
☞ cross (punch)

SUPLEX

Description

This high-arching takedown secures the opponent in a rear, front or side-body lock. The fighter then picks up his opponent and throws him backward, slamming him to the ground. A fighter will find his opponent's back to him through the fight's own dynamics or a specific technique like the arm drag or other wrestling maneuvers. The suplex is also known as the *souplesse*.

Application
General Suplex Scenario

1. Having secured a rear-body lock against Fighter B, Fighter A drops his center of gravity by bending at the knees a little.

2. He then explosively lifts Fighter B up, throwing his opponent over in a rainbowlike arcing motion. Note that Fighter A arches his back to achieve this motion.

3. This causes Fighter B to land hard on the back of his head, neck and shoulder.

4. After the suplex, Fighter A rolls Fighter B to the right.

Insight

- This move was best exemplified when Dan Severn applied it against Anthony Macias in the UFC 4, or when Kevin Randleman applied it against Fedor Emelianenko during a match at PRIDE: Critical Countdown 2004.

5-6. This transitions Fighter A into side control where he can ground-and-pound Fighter B.

Additional Information
☞ arm drag

SWITCH

Description

This reversal maneuver, which is derived from wrestling, can be applied from a number of different positions—standing, seating, bottom turtle, and from both front and back positions. The key elements to this maneuver are to scoot the hips away from the opponent and wedge the "switching" arm over the opponent's corresponding side arm and underneath his inner thigh to apply pressure to break free and reverse him.

Application
General Switch Scenario

1. Fighter B has Fighter A in a rear-body lock. To prevent him from immediately doing a takedown, Fighter A quickly traps his hands.

2. Fighter A scoots his hips as far away from Fighter B as possible.

3. From there, Fighter A wedges his right arm over Fighter B's right arm and underneath Fighter B's right inner thigh.

4. He then maintains the scooting-his-hips-away pressure and applies pressure to Fighter B's arm by sitting back into his opponent and pulling up with his right arm.

5. This synchronization of movements puts a lot of pressure on Fighter B's arms and hands thus enabling Fighter A to break the body lock. As his opponent's hold is broken, Fighter A sits his butt to the ground and pivots clockwise.

Insights

- A competitor can do a switch when back-to-back or face-to-face with his opponent.

- No matter the position, a fighter will use the tactic to reverse his position and obtain back control over his adversary.

6. Fighter A turns into Fighter B and reverses positions.

7. He now obtains the top-turtle position.

8. From this position, Fighter A goes on the offensive and can either transition into a back-control position or stand up.

Additional Information
☞ turtle position

TOEHOLD

Description

A toehold is a catch-as-catch-can wrestling technique that causes an opponent to submit or break his ankle. A fighter grasps the opponent's foot in a figure-4 hold, rotating it inwardly clockwise or counterclockwise, depending on which foot is captured. This technique is usually applied from side-control position or from inside the guard (top guard).

Application
General Toehold Scenario

1. From inside the closed guard, Fighter A grounds-and-pounds Fighter B with a left straight punch to the face.

2. He follows it with a left downward elbow strike to Fighter B's midsection.

3. These strikes break open Fighter B's closed guard.

4. As soon as its open, Fighter A posts his left knee and twists around to his left side, grabbing a toehold on Fighter B's right foot. He pushes the foot down.

Insight

- In the formative years of Pancrase and the UFC, this move was more commonly seen. It was also a favorite of Bas Rutten.

5. Upon securing the right foot, Fighter A immediately wraps his right arm over and under Fighter B's right calf, grasping his own wrist in a figure-4 hold.

6. Once this is secured, Fighter A quickly rotates Fighter B's foot clockwise, causing him to either submit or suffer a broken ankle.

Additional Information

☞ figure-4 holds
☞ side control
☞ top guard

TOP GUARD

Description

This position occurs when a fighter is inside an opponent's closed guard; he is "in the guard." It is a position in which he can execute the ground-and-pound tactic or a leg-lock submission hold to finish off an opponent. A top-guard fighter can also pass the bottom-positioned guard into side control or the mount, or disengage and stand up.

Applications
Top Guard From a Standing Position

1-2. In a standing top-guard position, Fighter A grounds-and-pounds Fighter B. He maintains a wide base for stability.

Top Guard From a Ground Position

1-3. From a based-out top-guard position, Fighter A uses elbow strikes and straight punches to keep Fighter B on the defensive. This keeps Fighter B preoccupied and unable to swiftly use his closed guard to transition into other techniques.

Additional Information
- ☞ closed guard
- ☞ passing the guard

TRIANGLE ARMBAR

Description

A competitor generally uses the triangle armbar if he doesn't successfully transition into a triangle choke. It is an opportunistic armbar that will submit an opponent. It is applied from a leg-triangle position.

Application
General Armbar Scenario

1. From a closed-guard position, Fighter A parries Fighter B's straight left punch.

2. While Fighter B throws an overhand right, Fighter A opens his guard.

3. Fighter A takes the opportunity to quickly maneuver his left leg over Fighter B's shoulder and around the back of Fighter B's neck.

4. While in the process of doing this, Fighter A grabs and immobilizes his opponent's left arm with his right hand.

Insights

- There are many variations of the triangle armbar. It is often applied as a "surprise" transitional submission hold from a triangle-choke attempt. It is a good technique to catch the opponent off-guard.

- It is important to have a tight leg triangle secured around the opponent's arm so that the hip fulcrum is utilized to its fullest extent and so that the opponent can't pull his arm out or create slack in his arm to nullify the hold.

Additional Information
☞ triangle choke

5. He immediately follows this up by placing the crook of his right knee on top of the crook of his left ankle, thus securing a leg-triangle position like in the triangle choke.

6. Fighter A then cinches the leg triangle by bending his right knee over his left ankle.

7. He pins Fighter B's left arm to the right side of his chest with both hands and hyperextends Fighter B's left elbow by thrusting his hips up to the ceiling.

8. Fighter B will either tap in submission or sustain a broken elbow.

TRIANGLE CHOKE

Description

This is one of the premier submission techniques to force an opponent to tap or be rendered unconscious. It is a leg-based blood choke in which the fighter encircles and constricts one of his legs around the opponent's neck, wrapping it up with his other leg in a figure-4 position while entangling one of his arms in the process. The choke is set by constricting the carotid artery on one side of the opponent's neck with one of the fighter's legs and his other carotid artery through the constriction of his own arm (via the fighter's encircled, wrapped leg). It is a versatile submission hold that can be executed from the guard, back-control or mount positions.

Applications
Triangle Choke From the Guard

1. From a top-guard position, Fighter B continues his ground-and-pound by throwing a left punch.

2. At that moment, Fighter A slides his right leg up and over Fighter B's left shoulder.

3. Upon doing so, he grabs the back of Fighter B's head and pulls it down to wrap his right leg around the back of Fighter B' neck.

4. As he bends and wraps his right leg around Fighter B's neck, Fighter A grabs and pulls Fighter B's right arm across his own chest.

5. To secure the hold, Fighter A grabs his right ankle to cinch the crook of his right knee tightly around the back of Fighter B's neck.

6. On cinching, Fighter A throws his left leg over his right ankle to hook the crook of his left knee over it.

7. Once this is set up, Fighter A squeezes his legs together and pulls down on Fighter B's head. If the choke is tightly locked, then Fighter B will tap or be rendered unconscious.

Insights

- The triangle choke is among the most effective, efficient and versatile submission holds in MMA (alongside the rear-naked choke and cross-body armbar). There are many variations and ways to set up and apply this choke, and it behooves any student of MMA to master this technique.

- To see this technique masterfully applied, watch Shinya Aoki (the undisputed MMA master when it comes to the triangle) and Miguel Torres. These fighters have applied this move against many different opponents successfully. Study these guys' fights to gain valuable fighting application insights on this technique.

- The triangle choke is technically a stranglehold or blood choke because it constricts blood flow in the carotid arteries rather than airflow.

Triangle Choke From a Supine Position

1. From a supine position with back control, Fighter A plans to apply a triangle choke.

2-3. He brings his right leg up and over Fighter B's right shoulder. Fighter A gives himself some stability to do this by maintaining his left leg on Fighter B's inner thigh and pushing Fighter B's head with his right hand.

4. He creates space to slide his right leg underneath Fighter B's armpit by pulling Fighter B's left arm across his opponent's body.

5. Fighter A cinches the crook of his right knee along Fighter B's neck and locks the hold by bending his left leg over his right ankle.

6. Fighter A constricts Fighter B's neck by squeezing his legs together and bending his left knee. Fighter B will have to tap out or be rendered unconscious within seconds.

Additional Information
- ☞ armbar
- ☞ guillotine choke
- ☞ kimura
- ☞ rear-naked choke

TURTLE POSITION (BOTTOM AND TOP)

Description

The bottom turtle is a passive, defensive position in which a competitor is on his elbows (or hands) and knees, while the top turtle is an active, offensive position in which a competitor is behind and off to one side (usually with the outside knee posted) of the bottom turtle-positioned opponent. The top turtle is free to get back control, blast his knees to the opponent's ribs, stand up to pummel his adversary or transition into other techniques like submissions. The fighter in a bottom-turtle position is extremely vulnerable and wants to get out of the position as quickly as possible.

Application
Top-Turtle Transition Into Back Control

1. Fighter A is in a top-turtle position with his outside knee posted. Fighter B is in a bottom-turtle position.

2. To put Fighter B into back control, Fighter A begins to grapevine his right foot around his opponent's right leg.

3. Fighter A inserts his right foot to hook Fighter B's inner thigh, securing a single grapevine.

4. With his right grapevine hooked in, Fighter A begins to "climb" up Fighter B's back to secure an underhook on his left arm.

Insights

- Turning one's back on an opponent is rarely, if ever, a good tactic, and taking a bottom-turtle position is no exception. A bottom-turtle fighter wants to get out of the position by standing up, rolling onto his back or putting the top-turtle opponent in his guard as quickly as possible.

- Because I have shown the more dominant prone back-control position in other techniques, the example I provided for this term involved maneuvering the bottom-turtle opponent into a supine position.

- In the UFC 83, Georges St. Pierre caught Matt Serra in a bottom turtle. He blasted Serra's ribs with knee strikes until the referee stepped in to stop the fight.

Additional Information
☞ back control
☞ grapevines

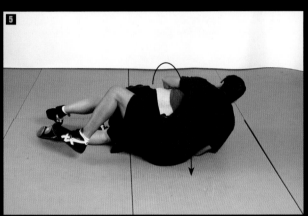

5. He then uses the underhook on Fighter B's left armpit to pull them both into a supine position.

6. As he does this, Fighter A wraps his right arm around Fighter B's right shoulder and neck. This gives Fighter A head-and-arm control of his opponent while supine.

7. With both competitors supine, Fighter A makes sure to have a double grapevine.

8. Having secured back control, Fighter A has the option of finishing Fighter B off with a rear-naked choke.

UNDERHOOKS

Description

Like overhooks, underhooks are wrestling-based tie-up arm positions used offensively and defensively in a clinch. They are also used to set up or thwart takedowns, for dirty boxing tactics and ground grappling/fighting control.

Applications
Takedown Defense With Underhooks

1. Fighter A has double-arm underhooks on Fighter B's right and left arms while in the clinch position.

2. Fighter B attempts a double-leg takedown.

3. But Fighter A is able to use the underhooks, in conjunction with a sprawl, as a barrier between Fighter B's arms and his own legs.

- As mentioned in the description, underhooks are used both offensively and defensively in a number of ways. It is useful in controlling an opponent and transitioning into an offensive maneuver. Defensively, it is invaluable in thwarting takedown attempts and maneuvering into more advantageous positions.

Takedown Setup With Underhooks

1-2. Fighter A uses his underhooks as a means to transition into a body-lock position in order to execute a body-lock takedown.

Additional Information
☞ body-lock takedowns
☞ overhooks

UP-KICK

Description

This upward-thrusting kick is delivered from the shell position to the head or body of an upright opponent. It is a powerful strike, which a fighter uses to stand up or knockout the standing opponent.

Application
Up-Kick From the Shell Position

1. Fighter B stands close to Fighter A, who is in the shell position. Fighter B throws a diving overhand punch to Fighter A's face.

Insights

- This is a potent knockout kick to utilize from the shell position. From Renzo Gracie's up-kick knockout of Oleg Taktarov at the Martial Arts Reality Superfighting event in 1996 to Gegard Mousasi's up-kick knockout of Ronaldo Souza for the middleweight Grand Prix 2008 Championship at DREAM 6, the up-kick has proved its value in MMA and is an excellent kick to have in a fighter's MMA arsenal.

- UFC allows body up-kicks only, but DREAM allows up-kicks to the head.

2. Fighter A shoots up a left up-kick by thrusting his foot upward and straight to and through Fighter B's chin.

Additional Information
☞ shell position

UPPERCUT (PUNCH)

Description

The uppercut is a close-range boxing-based punch that travels in an oblique (vertically upward) trajectory. It can be delivered with either hand with the primary targets being the chin and solar plexus. The uppercut is a potent punch to use when applying the dirty boxing clinch or in conjunction with hooks.

Application
General Uppercut Scenarios

1. Fighter A lands a left uppercut to Fighter B's solar plexus.

2. Fighter A lands a right uppercut to Fighter B's chin. This is a knockout blow.

Insights

- The rear uppercut to the head is the most prevalently used version of the punch in MMA (as well as in boxing) and is known as a potent knockout blow when landed "on the button" (boxing parlance for "on the chin").

- The rear uppercut to the body comes in second in terms of usage.

- The lead uppercut, whether to the head or body, is used more sparingly with the lead hook being the predominant "go-to" close-range punch because of its better feel, flow and power.

- Like any punch, the uppercut requires proper punching form—chin tucked, hands up, elbows in, knees slightly bent, good body balance, striking through the target, and exhaling on execution for power as well as a quick retraction.

3. Fighter A lands a left uppercut to Fighter B's chin from a dirty boxing clinch.

Additional Information
☞ hook (punch)

WHIZZER

Description

A whizzer is an upright wrestling maneuver in which a fighter thwarts a takedown or clinch by overhooking an opponent's armpit. The fighter then twists his adversary around himself in order to gain a more advantageous position. As he twists, the fighter wrenches his trapped arm away from his opponent. A typical whizzer "finish" involves driving the opponent's overhooked shoulder to the ground.

Applications
Whizzer Against a Single-Leg Takedown

1. Fighter B shoots in for a single-leg takedown, which Fighter A counters with a quarter nelson and hooks his right foot outside of Fighter B's left outer thigh.

2. He breaks Fighter B's hold by applying downward pressure with the quarter nelson and kicking back with his right leg. This leaves him with an overhook on Fighter B's arm.

3. He whips Fighter B to the left with a whizzer.

4. This breaks Fighter B's hold. Fighter A continues the wrenching and whipping motion, which is augmented by an explosive twist of the hips.

5. This drives Fighter B to the ground in a prone position from which Fighter A can either stay in side control to ground-and-pound or transition into back control to ground-and-pound.

Insights

- The whizzer is an overhook that is used offensively or defensively with a whipping, wrenching twist of the arm and hips to displace an opponent's position into one that is more disadvantageous.

- Like with underhooks, it is vitally important to learn and master the overhooks in all its variants, including the potent whizzer maneuver.

Whizzer in a Clinch

1. Fighter A and Fighter B are in a clinch. Fighter A overhooks Fighter B's right arm (not shown).

2. Fighter A applies the whizzer by whipping Fighter B in a clockwise direction.

3. This off-balances Fighter B, putting him in a disadvantageous position long enough for Fighter A to strike him.

4. Fighter A blasts him with an uppercut to the chin.

5. He follows up with a knee strike to the head.

Additional Information

☞ overhooks
☞ quarter nelson

WRESTLING CLINCH

Description

This clinch uses both arms to pummel an opponent through underhooking, overhooking and body locking to secure double underhooks. From here, the fighter can perform a body-lock or other takedowns.

Application
General Wrestling Clinch Scenario

1-8. This sequence tries to convey the dynamism of two combatants pummeling with overhooks and underhooks to obtain an advantageous position over the other. It ends with Fighter A obtaining double underhooks against Fighter B's double overhooks.

Insights

- The wrestling clinch is an integral part of the MMA game.

- It behooves all MMA fighters to learn and understand the subtleties and nuances of this clinch so a fighter can use it against his opponent and not have it used against him.

Additional Information

☞ overhooks
☞ pummeling
☞ underhooks

MIXED MARTIAL ARTS RESOURCES

Books

These books are worth checking out if you are interested in learning more about the tactical and technical details of mixed martial arts.

Overall

Bas Rutten's Big Book of Combat, Volumes 1 & 2 by Bas Rutten and Stephen Quadros. Mixed Martial Arts LLC (2002).

Brazilian Jiu-Jitsu No Holds Barred! Fighting Techniques by Rodrigo Gracie and Kid Peligro. Invisible Cities Press (2005).

Fedor: The Fighting System of the World's Undisputed King of MMA by Glen Cordoza, Fedor Emilianenko and Erich Krauss. Victory Belt Publishing (2008).

Fighter's Notebook: A Manual of Mixed Martial Arts by Kirik Jenness and David Roy. Bench Pr Intl (1998).

Mixed Martial Arts: The Book of Knowledge by B.J. Penn, Glen Cordoza and Erich Krauss. Victory Belt Publishing (2007).

The Ultimate Guide to Mixed Martial Arts. Black Belt Books (2007).

Striking

Boxing Mastery: Advanced Technique, Tactics and Strategies From the Sweet Science by Mark Hatmaker and Doug Werner. Tracks Publishing (2004).

Boxing's Ten Commandments: Essential Training for the Sweet Science by Alan Lachica and Doug Werner. Tracks Publishing (2007).

Fighting Strategies of Muay Thai: Secrets of Thailand's Boxing Camps by Mark Van Schuyver and Pedro Solana Villalobos. Paladin Press (2002).

Mixed Martial Arts Instruction Manual: Striking by Anderson Silva, Erich Krauss and Glen Cordoza. Victory Belt Publishing (2008).

Muay Thai Unleashed by Erich Krauss. McGraw-Hill (2006).

No Holds Barred Fighting: The Kicking Bible by Mark Hatmaker. Tracks Publishing (2008).

No Holds Barred Fighting: Savage Strikes by Mark Hatmaker. Tracks Publishing (2004).

Grappling

Brazilian Jiu-Jitsu Fighting Strategies by Romero Cavalcanti and Mark Van Schuyver. Paladin Press (2006).

Brazilian Jiu-Jitsu: The Master Text by Gene Simco. Jiu-Jitsu.net (2001).

Brazilian Jiu-Jitsu Submission Grappling Techniques by Royler Gracie and Kid Peligro. Invisible Cities Press (2003).

The Guard: Brazilian Jiu-Jitsu Details and Techniques by Joe Moreira and Ed Beneville. Grappling Arts Publications (2009).

Greco-Roman Wrestling by William A. Martell. Human Kinetics Publishers (1993).

Judo for Mixed Martial Arts by Karo Parisyan, Erich Krauss and Glen Cordoza. Victory Belt Publishing (2008).

Mastering Jujitsu by Renzo Gracie and John Danaher. Human Kinetics Publishers (2003).

Mastering Mixed Martial Arts: The Guard by Antonio Rodrigo Nogueira, Erich Krauss and Glen Cordoza. Victory Belt Publishing (2008).

More No Holds Barred Fighting: Killer Submissions by Mark Hatmaker and Doug Werner. Tracks Publishing (2003).

No Holds Barred Fighting: The Clinch by Mark Hatmaker. Tracks Publishing (2006).

No Holds Barred Fighting: Takedowns by Mark Hatmaker. Tracks Publishing (2005).

No Holds Barred Fighting: The Ultimate Guide to Submission Wrestling by Mark Hatmaker and Doug Werner. Tracks Publishing (2000).

Passing the Guard: Brazilian Jiu-Jitsu Details and Techniques by Ed Beneville and Tim Cartmell. Grappling Arts Publications (2009).

Strategic Guard: Brazilian Jiu-Jitsu: Details and Techniques by Joe Moreira and Ed Beneville. Grappling Arts Publications (2008).

Training for Competition: Brazilian Jiu-Jitsu and Submission Grappling by David Meyer. Black Belt Books (2008).

Ultimate Fighting Techniques Volume 1: The Top Game by Royce Gracie and Kid Peligro. Invisible Cities Press (2004).

Ultimate Fighting Techniques Volume 2: Fighting From the Bottom by Royce Gracie and Kid Peligro. Invisible Cities Press (2006).

The Ultimate Guide to Grappling. Black Belt Books (2007).

Winning Wrestling Moves by Mark Mynsk, Barry Davis and Brook Simpson. Human Kinetics Publishers (1994).

Wrestling for Fighting: The Natural Way by Randy Couture, Erich Krauss and Glen Cordoza. Victory Belt Publishing (2007).

Video/DVD Instructional Series

These instructional DVDs impart an overall, integrated grasp of mixed-martial arts skills.

Bas Rutten's Big DVDs of Combat (7 DVDs)

Cross Training with Shonie Carter (7 DVDs)

Learn to Fight and Win with Pat Miletich (6 DVDs)

Mixed Martial Arts: The Conditioning Series with Chuck Liddell (7 DVDs)

Mixed Martial Arts: The Conditioning Series with Tito Ortiz (7 DVDs)

My Mixed Martial Arts with Denis Kang (1 DVD)

Secrets of Chute Boxe with Mauricio "Shogun" Rua and Murilo "Ninja" Rua (6 DVDs)

Ultimate Grappling with Chris Brennan, Shonie Carter, Ze Mario Esfiha, Alan Goes, Ricardo Teixeira

Ultimate MMA with Chuck Liddell and Tito Ortiz (12 DVDs)

Ultimate Stand Up with Shonie Carter, Rob McCullough and Vincent Soberano (8 DVDs)

Ultimate Street Fighting with Ricardo de la Riva (4 DVDs)

Ultimate Takedowns with Kevin Jackson and Mike Van Arsdale (6 DVDs)

Vale Tudo Series 1: Vale-Tudo Takedowns with Mario Sperry (6 DVDs)

Vale Tudo Series 2: Advanced Vale-Tudo Takedowns with Mario Sperry and Murilo Bustamante (6 DVDs)

Vale Tudo Series 3: Striking and Takedowns with Mario Sperry (6 DVDs)

Web Sites

News sites give constant updates on fights, fighter statuses, upcoming events and other interesting stories. If you want to buy MMA gear, check out the equipment sites. For more MMA sites, try Google.

News

Cage Potato
www.cagepotato.com

Mixed Martial Arts.com
www.mixedmartialarts.com

MMA Fighting
www.mmafighting.com

MMA Junkie
mmajunkie.com

MMA Weekly
www.mmaweekly.com

Sherdog
www.sherdog.com

Ultimate Fighting Championship
www.ufc.com

Yahoo MMA
http://sports.yahoo.com/mma

Resources

Fight Authority
www.fightauthority.com

Fight Resource
www.fightresource.com

Supplies

Asian World of Martial Arts
www.awma.com

Century Martial Arts
www.centurymartialarts.com

Combat Sports
www.combatsports.com

Ringside Boxing
www.ringside.com

Title Boxing
www.titleboxing.com

GLOSSARY

Air choke: See choke.

Basing out: To maintain side control and make the position more stable, a fighter bases out by spreading his legs. If done properly, his legs should look like two sides of a triangle.

Blood choke: Also known as a stranglehold, a blood choke constricts the carotid arteries and cuts off blood flow to the brain.

Bucking: To escape a mount, a fighter can buck his opponent by thrusting his hips upward to knock his opponent off-balance.

Choke: This submission constricts the windpipe and cuts off oxygen to the brain.

Circling footwork: During a stand-up encounter, if the fighter is on the opponent's right side, he circles clockwise. If the fighter is on the opponent's left side, he circles counterclockwise.

The deck: The mat or the ground.

Dirty Boxing: Using boxing strikes while clinching an opponent's neck. The dirty boxing clinch is a component of dirty boxing, just as the *muay Thai* clinch is part of the art of muay Thai.

In the guard: When a fighter is caught inside an opponent's closed guard, he is considered in the guard. It is better known as top guard.

Knees-on-deck position: When a fighter's knees are on the ground, he's in the knees-on-deck position.

Lead foot: During stand-up, the lead foot is the foot that's closer to the opponent.

Lead hand: During stand-up, the lead hand is the hand that's closer to the opponent. Most fighters lead with their weaker hand and use it to set up power attacks.

Matched Lead: During a stand-up encounter, fighters are in the matched lead when they're in the same stance and have the same foot forward.

Posting: Many techniques are easier for a fighter to perform when a fighter posts by pressing either a limb or his head to the mat for support. Doing so improves his balance and center of gravity.

Prone: When a fighter is either on the mat or on his hands and knees, he is considered prone when he is facing downward.

Rear foot: During stand-up, the rear foot refers to the foot that's farther away from the opponent. Because the rear foot has to travel farther to reach its target, its attacks are more powerful and difficult to pull off.

Rear hand: During stand-up, the rear hand refers to the hand that's farther away from the opponent. Because the rear hand has to travel farther to reach its target, its attacks are more powerful and difficult to pull off.

Shrimping: When on the ground, a fighter can shrimp by turning his hips to the side to create enough space to escape his attacker.

Supine: A fighter is supine when he is lying on his back and facing upward.

Stranglehold: See blood choke.

Trapping: To protect against and set up attacks, a fighter traps a part of the opponent's body by immobilizing it with a grappling technique.

Tie-up maneuver: To control a standing opponent, a fighter clinches his opponent's neck with a single hand.

Unmatched Lead: During a stand-up encounter, fighters are in the unmatched lead when they're in opposite stances, meaning one fighter is leading with his right foot and the other is leading with his left.

INDEX

ABOUT THE AUTHOR

Lito Angeles is an avid martial arts researcher, writer, practitioner and instructor who began training in 1975. Over the ensuing years, he has studied *shorin-ryu* karate, *jeet kune do, kali, escrima*, Western boxing, Western wrestling, *muay Thai, pentjak silat, boxe Francaise savate, krav maga,* Brazilian *jiu-jitsu* and the Real Combat System. He has attained instructor/coach credentials in several of the aforementioned systems and is the U.S. chief instructor of renowned U.K. martial artist Geoff Thompson's Real Combat System.

He is a 20-year veteran police officer with a Southern California police department and a contributing writer for *Black Belt* since 1998. He indulges in his passion for martial arts by continually studying and training, teaching privately, conducting seminars and writing books and articles.